£2.99

J Cleland
Scarborough summer 2004

THE
ROYAL FAMILY
IN
WARTIME

By gracious permission of His Majesty the King, the Council of King George's Jubilee Trust have been authorized to prepare this record of THE ROYAL FAMILY IN WARTIME.

The Council express their cordial thanks to Lord Southwood, Chairman of Odhams Press Ltd., for producing this book and for devoting the whole of the proceeds to the funds of the Trust.

DURING LONDON'S ORDEAL

THE
ROYAL FAMILY
IN
WARTIME

THE ILLUSTRATED STORY
OF THE ACTIVITIES OF THE
ROYAL FAMILY IN THE SERVICE
OF PEOPLE AND EMPIRE

1945

ODHAMS PRESS LIMITED · LONG ACRE · LONDON · W · C · 2

SCEPTRE AND SWORD

ONE of " Q's " novels has for its central figure a little girl of six, who comes home to her father in England after having been brought up from babyhood in the United States. Directly she lands she begins to ask questions about Windsor Castle, " because that is where the King lives. I used to call him *my* King over on the Other Side, because my name is Corona, and means I was born the year he was crowned. They make out they don't hold much stock in kings, back there; but that sort of talk didn't take me in, because when you *have* a king of your own you know what it feels like." Corona speaks for most of her inarticulate elders all over the British Empire. We know that some of our best friends in the modern world—the Americans, the French, the Russians—hold little stock in kings, and conduct their affairs successfully without them. It is good for us to be reminded that a satisfactory social and political order can be organized in other ways than ours. But respect for the achievement of these great republics does not alter our inner conviction that monarchy is, if not the best system in all times and places, at any rate the best for us. We know " what it feels like to have a king," and we should feel exceedingly unhappy without him.

For most of us, most of the time, the instinctive feeling of rightness in giving our loyalty to a king is enough. But of course there are solid reasons for our system, if we choose to consider them. An institution that has held the English people together for a thousand years—when we tried for a short time to dispense with a king, government quickly broke down—is evidently founded on something more than sentiment. It might, indeed, be argued that the gulf between Alfred the Great, proclaiming his laws to the scanty people he ruled in a few beleaguered shires round Winchester, and George VI, who does not in any direct sense rule at all, but who speaks on Christmas Day from his study to a quarter of the world's population, scattered from Quebec to Melbourne, and from Colombo to Aberdeen, is so vast as to take all coherent meaning from the title that they share. Certainly the

idea of kingship has changed unceasingly through the centuries—which is another way of saying that it is a living and growing thing. But the more it is studied the more it is found that its essence is permanent, answering to some permanent need in human nature, and especially in British nature.

Historians tell us that the first English kings were the leaders of the Anglo-Saxon war bands who overran our country on the fall of the Roman Empire—in other words, that a king is a glorified commander-in-chief. Something of that idea undoubtedly survives today. The King is in a very special sense the head of all the fighting services: they wear his uniform, they take his " shilling," his name is constantly before them as the very centre of their duty and devotion. He is Admiral of the Fleet, Field-Marshal, Marshal of the Royal Air Force. Nevertheless, it would be strange if our great peace-loving Empire conceived of its head as a war lord. There is a great deal more in the idea of a King of England than that.

What we certainly do not understand by a king is the possessor of supreme power. For 300 years the power of the King to control government has been growing steadily less, until today he does not personally rule at all, but merely lends his name to the Ministers, responsible to the elected representatives of the people, who wield the effective authority. Yet for at least the last century the significance of the monarchy in the popular mind has been growing greater and greater, until now, when his legal powers have reached their lowest point, the place of the King in the hearts of his many peoples is more secure than ever before. Many foreign observers are puzzled to understand how we can give so exalted a place in the order of our life to a personage to whom we concede so little executive authority. But in fact there is a deep significance in the apparent paradox. By giving the highest place in the Empire to a man who is not the most powerful, we proclaim our belief, which contains a good deal of the secret of our political success, that there are more important things in our national life than power. The King represents

REVIEWING BRITAIN'S NAVAL MIGHT

WITH THE WAR CABINET. *Above is snown the War Cabinet of the All-Party Government, dissolved in May, 1945. (Left to right) Mr. Morrison (Home Office), Lord Woolton (Reconstruction),*

those things, and therefore the possessors of power are expected to treat him with the utmost deference. Commanders-in-Chief stand to attention and salute; Prime Ministers " present their humble duty " and respectfully explain their policies. The humility thus enjoined upon our effective rulers is one of the great safeguards against their becoming inflated into dictators.

But if the King stands for ideas that lie beyond power, it is still necessary to consider what these ideas are. Perhaps another glance into the dim past will throw some light upon them. If we turn from the historians to the anthropologists, whose business it is to explore the workings of the mind of primitive man, they will tell us that the first kings, distinguishable before the dawn of history, were neither soldiers nor politicians, but magical personalities. In every tribe a consecrated being was set apart, whose life was obscurely believed to be in some sort the life of the whole community, and of the crops by which it lived. While the magical king remained strong and

Sir John Anderson (Exchequer), Mr. Attlee (Deputy Prime Minister), H.M. the King, Mr. Churchill (Prime Minister), Mr. Eden (Foreign Affairs), Mr. Lyttelton (Production), and Mr. Bevin (Labour)

healthy, the corn would grow abundantly and the tribe would prosper in peace and war; if he was weakly or ailing, the harvest would fail, and the tribe would be in danger of conquest by its enemies.

We have shaken ourselves free from the superstitions in which these primitive kings had their origin. But we have not been released from human nature; and we still feel the instinctive needs to which they answered. The more strongly we are conscious of our community life, the more necessary we feel it to have a symbol of that life. This is true of all peoples, whether they live under a monarchy or a republic. Some seem able to content themselves with an abstract idea, a document, or an emblem; the Frenchman has his "Liberty, Equality, Fraternity"; the American has the Constitution, or "Old Glory." The British peoples believe that the immemorial idea of a man set apart to represent the life of the people has richer, more human, more versatile potentialities than any of the abstractions. We have

UNITED NATIONS' PARADE, 1942

come to think of the King as the supremely representative man, the most English Englishman, the most British member of the British Empire. We expect him to set an example of living in the English manner, to live the normal English life at its best, as we should all like to live it if all of us could have the scope and spaciousness that are possible to royalty, and to live that life to a large extent in public, so that every one can feel that in a sense he shares in it. And since the fullest natural life of an Englishman is a home life, with his wife at his side and his family growing up round him, there is an indispensable part for the Queen and her children to play in fulfilling the royal task of representative living.

Now, since we all, high and low, rich and poor, in all parts of the world-wide Empire, accept this one man as our supreme type and pattern, we are enabled through our relation to him to feel our national and imperial unity more intensely. In all that the King says or does, he speaks and acts for the people; and when we are given laws or receive orders in his name, it is the people incarnate in him that we obey. When, for instance, a new Government has to be formed, its head is, as a rule, clearly designated by the party that possesses a majority in the House of Commons. Nevertheless, the leader of that party, on becoming Prime Minister, receives his trust from the King, who stands not for the majority but for the whole people, and for that reason the Minister is expected to govern with an eye to the interests of us all, and not merely of his own supporters. All who serve in the armed forces or in official employment " under the Crown," as the constitutional phrase goes, similarly make their profession of loyalty to the King, which is only another way of saying that they serve the whole people. The judges in the courts, sitting with the royal arms over their heads, administer " the King's justice," that is, the justice that has been developed according to the immemorial customs of the people, modified from age to age to fit the changing circumstances of the world.

In two special ways the uniting influence of the King is fundamental to the British way of life. He stands for our unity both in space and in time. In space, because all the diverse communities of the British Commonwealth and Empire, scattered all round the globe, look to him in exactly the same way as do his subjects in the British

Isles; and now that the great self-governing Dominions, to which we hope India will soon be added, have outgrown all subordination to the government at Westminster, the person of the King is the sole visible link that holds the Commonwealth together. The King is further a uniting influence in time. George VI is connected by blood with all the past sovereigns of England— with George V and Queen Victoria; with George III, who received the trophies of Trafalgar and Waterloo; with Queen Anne, who welcomed home the victor of Blenheim; with Elizabeth, for whom Shakespeare wrote his plays and Drake won his battles, and also with her rival, Mary Stewart; with Henry, the hero of Agincourt and Edward, the victor of Crecy; with Edward I, who established the foundations of Parliament, as well as with Robert the Bruce; with Richard Lionheart, who led the great Crusade; with William the Conqueror and Alfred the Great, and the half-legendary kings of Wessex who presided over the misty beginnings of the English story. It is our hope that his descendants will still reign from Windsor to Wellington for centuries after we are gone. It is the King who stands in the national life for the unity of times past and times to come; his presence at the head of all branches of public life sets the endless adventure of government, which is after all a romantic affair, against its worthy background, the long vista of ancestral glories and future hopes, and reminds us all of the grandeur of the historic succession in which our generation stands.

In times of urgent danger such as those through which the nation, with the Commonwealth and Empire, has just passed, a people has need of all these kinds of unity, carried to their highest possible pitch, if it is to hold fast and survive. At each testing moment of these terrible years we have required to feel, and we have felt, that we are all moulded into one brotherhood by the greatness of a challenge that transcends our differences of rank or function—sailors, soldiers and airmen welded into a single instrument of war, the field-marshal and the private fighting the same battle for the same victory, the fighter pilot overhead and the rescue worker digging in the ruins both part of the same defence system, the factory hand, the housewife and the administrative official all allies in keeping the wheels of civilian life turning so that the machine of the war effort shall not falter. If we can say that all these things are done " for the King," we translate the abstract idea of national unity into terms of living personality that are immediately intelligible to our hearts, and are helped to see all our battles and our labours as parts of one gigantic task, shared out among us all according to our capacities of service.

No less important has it been in the war years to be conscious of the bond that unites the British communities all round the globe. In those dark days of 1940, when we stood alone, we should have had little hope of maintaining our resistance to the all-conquering hosts of Germany without the confidence that the invisible links of sea-power round the world would be held firm by the spontaneous loyalty of the great Dominions beyond the oceans. While the people of the British Isles were defying the Luftwaffe, and at the same time sending abroad their small resources of armour to begin the counter-offensive in the Mediterranean, Canadians were pouring into England to reinforce the defence, Australians and New Zealanders were manning the critical land-bridges between east and west, and South Africans were sweeping the Italians out of Africa. Side by side with them fought the martial races of India; while from all the scattered dependencies where the flag flies volunteers came flocking to the colours and free gifts in aid of the common cause poured in. To one of these dependencies, the heroic island of Malta, fell the honour of a defence more critical for the strategy of the whole Empire than was allotted to any other community of comparable numbers; and the world knows with what superb valour the trust was discharged. These splendid services to the cause of liberty were not inspired by any sentiment of loyalty to England. The Dominions are sovereign nations, in every aspect of status equal with Great Britain, and India and the Colonies look forward to the day when they shall enjoy similar independence of control by the British Government. The loyalty of them all is offered to something much larger than England or Great Britain, to the idea of a free family of self-governing nations; but for them all the head of the family is the King. It is because they all look to one man as the focus of their allegiance and their affection that they possessed in 1939 and

AT GEORGE CROSS ISLAND. *A huge crowd demonstrates the triumphant spirit of Malta as the King appears on the balcony of the Palace at Valetta, capital of the island, during his visit in 1943*

1940 their unique capacity to act together, and by their united action to save the world.

Thirdly, the spiritual strength that enabled the British people to confront, without doubt or dismay, the power by which all Europe had been overwhelmed, was surely drawn in no small measure from the sense that they fought in defence of something more permanent than the fortunes of one fleeting generation of men.

In our halls is hung
Armoury of the invincible knights of old.

There was a sacred trust to be discharged; an inheritance handed down through endless generations, which must be preserved intact against no matter what peril, in order to be passed on undiminished to posterity. It was for the immortality of England and the Empire that their sons offered their mortal lives; and the representative of that immortality was the King, the descendant of those who had typified the ancient glories, the ancestor of sovereigns under whom new glories will be won.

But of all these aspects of unity, the unity of the people in their struggle against despotism, the unity of the nations of the Commonwealth in their defence of the ideals they share, the unity of the past, the present, and the future of the race, the King is the representative, and not merely the symbol. He is not an abstraction, like the Crown or the flag or the constitution, but a living, breathing man, whose task it is to make actually visible or audible to all his subjects the great ideas for which he stands. It is the King's function always to personify the whole in relation to the parts, to remind each individual fighting or working or suffering in the service of the war effort that he is a member of a vast community, and that the whole community is interested in how he —or she—plays his part. When cabinets or chiefs of staff or commanders-in-chief have perfected large plans for the defence of a capital or the invasion of a continent, they bring them to the King for his assent—not because the King can be expected to have the technical knowledge to add to the designs of the specialists, but because the King's approval is that of the whole people whom Ministers of State and admirals and generals are appointed to serve. When a fleet or an army or a combined force operating in the modern manner by sea, land and air, is about to set out upon an expedition of great import, the King goes among them to wish them God speed, because he is the one man who has in him authority to bring them messages of love and confidence on behalf of all their friends and countrymen, each one of whom would wish to deliver his message himself, but is proud to be represented instead by a royal deputy. When valour or devoted service has to be rewarded, it is the King who pins on the medal, and thereby conveys to the winner of it the thanks of all his subjects for the deeds that have been done in the cause of them all. Wherever there is arduous war work to be done, or a weary watch to be kept, a visit from the King or the Queen reminds the workers and the watchers that their service is an indispensable part of a task in which the whole nation is engaged, and on which the fate of the whole depends. When there has been suffering, or loss, or bereavement, at the bedside of the wounded, in ruins of bombed homes, over and over again the King or the Queen or some member of the Royal Family has been quickly on the spot; and their words of quick sympathy have meant, not only that their own hearts are moved, but that through them a nation united in feeling, as in service, would wish to express its sorrow at an injury by which all are afflicted. When at critical phases of the struggle, or on solemn anniversaries, such as Christmas Day, words of exhortation or comfort had to be addressed to the whole people, no broadcast could be so representative or so immediately acceptable as the King's. And finally, at the end of it all, when triumph had been achieved by the united efforts of the Empire and its allies, the cheers of the vast multitudes outside Buckingham Palace on victory day, and the answering salutes from the balcony, the mutual greetings of King and people, were the symbolic declaration that it was the spirit of unity, for which the King stands, that had won the war.

But the King is only one man. It is just because he is only one that he can represent the nation's unity. He is head of Church and State, supreme commander of all the armed services, the head of the judiciary, the fountain of honour. As Emperor of India, King of Canada, Australia, New Zealand, South Africa, he wears a cluster of crowns. But he has no more than the physical powers of a single human being; and there are only twenty-four hours even in a royal day. To carry through the multifarious tasks that the

WITH AUSTRALIAN TROOPS IN THE EASTERN COMMAND

intense life of a nation at war lays upon the sovereign and his family is almost a superhuman undertaking; it can only be accomplished by the most tireless and laborious devotion in the King himself, and, be it added, with the aid of what has never been wanting—a universal sympathy and good will among his subjects. Owing to the dangers of a life-and-death struggle with a ruthless adversary, much secrecy has had to surround, throughout the war, the movements of His Majesty. He has gone to and fro among his subjects with little of the publicity that would attend him in peace; his coming could not be heralded in advance, and his doings could be but vaguely recorded afterwards. Though all must

have been aware that he was ceaselessly active, and though he, perhaps, met face to face more of his subjects of all degrees than could have expected to see him in time of peace, the nature of his life in wartime England, and among his subjects and fighting men overseas, has been but dimly apprehended. Thousands of men and women have laboured in silence for six years before the nature of their vital service could be revealed to their countrymen ; and of these, too, the King is the representative. In the following pages some attempt is made to tell a connected story of the life of the Royal Family, and especially of His Majesty King George VI, during nearly six years of the German war.

NORTH AFRICA, 1943

BROADCASTING TO BRITAIN AND THE EMPIRE

IN THE SERVICE OF THE PEOPLE

ON May 12, 1937, the King and Queen were crowned in Westminster Abbey, and the Archbishop of Canterbury prayed over them that their people might have peace and prosperity in their time. But he also invested the King with the sword of justice, and prayed that he should not bear it in vain. To some of us who were present the ancient words seemed full of immediate import; for the European horizon was already dark with impending storm. The guns were booming in Spain; and beyond the Rhine the National Socialist Government was piling up armament and training a new generation of Germans in a fanatical devotion to the spirit of war. There were not many as yet to listen to the ex-Minister, Winston Churchill, now long out of office, when he told them that these things were an imminent threat to the very existence of the British Empire. But at least it was apparent that there were anxious times ahead, and something more than mere courtesy made it desirable that the new Sovereigns should introduce themselves to their country's closest friends. Soon in the year after they were crowned the King and Queen paid a visit to France, the staunch ally that had shared victory with the England of King George V; and as in that golden summer of 1938—while Hitler was preparing his assault on Czechoslovakia—they drove through cheering crowds down the lordly boulevards of Paris, French hearts opened to them, and through them seemed to renew something of the old intimacy with their people. The dire days that were to follow in less than two years, when England and France should be shorn asunder by the German scythe, were then beyond imagining; but looking back now, we may feel sure that, in the long years that France lay prostrate under the enemy's heel, those July days were many a time remembered, and the hearts of Frenchmen steeled to a more resolute resistance by the message of friendship unbreakable by adversity that the King and Queen of England had brought.

A year passed; and now Hitler was in Prague and the rumblings of war could no longer be disregarded by any one. Great Britain was rearming in haste, and young men, for the first time in what was still called peace, were being conscripted for military training. Carrying on the process begun in Paris, the King and Queen undertook a more extended mission, across the Atlantic instead of the Channel, which had a similar effect, whether consciously designed or not, in closing the ranks so soon to be assailed. It was about this time that Australia made a signal declaration of solidarity with all British peoples under the Crown by asking for the King's brother, the Duke of Kent, to be sent out to Canberra as Governor General. The King's consent, immediately and cordially given, was to be tragically prevented from ever taking effect. Their Majesties left England on May 6, and returned on June 22. During that time they toured the length and breadth of the vast Dominion of Canada, receiving the most moving demonstrations of loyalty alike from the population of British and of French descent, and by their presence helping Canadians to realize, not merely their links with the Commonwealth, but even their unity among themselves, which in so scattered a people is not always easy to preserve.

From Canada, in response to a pressing invitation, the King and Queen went on for a brief visit to the United States; and there the traditional American prejudice against the institution of monarchy melted away in the warm humanity of the people's welcome. To judge from the enthusiasm of the American press at the time, the triumph belonged in a special sense to the Queen, whose charm made a universal and instant appeal to the hearts of Americans. They stayed with President Roosevelt at his country home, and laid the foundations of a personal friendship with that great man and his wife, which were to be of the utmost importance to the United Nations in the grim years to come. Though King and President were not destined to meet again face to face, the understanding and mutual respect that continued to link them personally formed one of the earliest strands in the skein of association that was to be woven ever more closely between their countries by the experience of war.

ABOARD H.M.S. *ROYAL OAK*, SUNK AT SCAPA FLOW, 1939

These tours lie in time outside the war years; but no account of the service rendered by the Royal Family in wartime could leave them unmentioned. The thousands of miles of travel and incessant public appearance had been an exhausting ordeal, and the King and Queen had well earned the holiday that they sought with their children at Balmoral soon after their return. The thunder-clouds, however, were now gathering black over Europe; many thousands of their subjects were to have their holidays grimly interrupted in that autumn of mounting catastrophe, and there was to be no exception for royalty. The King was called south on August 8 to review the ships and men of the Reserve Fleet, assembled in Weymouth Bay. In outward form

it was a peace-time occasion; but Hitler was hurling threats against Poland, whose integrity the King's Government had guaranteed, and the chances were growing hourly less that the veteran seamen the King had come to meet, most of them wearing the medal ribbons of the last great war, would be able to return to their peaceful avocations with the merchant or the fishing fleet for many a perilous month to come. The King inspected his ships, walked the quarter-decks, visited the mess-decks and talked to the men, finding everywhere the quiet confidence of the Navy that, whatever challenge might come, the ancient staunchness of sea power would hold fast, the perpetual guarantee of Britain's safety. It was the first of several thousands of such visits that the

King was to pay to the fighting and labouring hosts who were already marshalling for the second world war.

He returned to Balmoral, to family life and the beginning of the shooting season; but there was less and less time to be devoted to his gun, and more and more to the telegrams and dispatches piling up on his desk, conveying ever more ominous messages. On August 23 the King had news from Mr. Neville Chamberlain, the Prime Minister, which convinced him that there could be no more thought of holiday making. Ribbentrop was in Moscow to sign the non-aggression pact which isolated Poland and placed her strategically at Germany's mercy; and the King of England hastened back to his capital, to find his Ministers contemplating all but inevitable war.

In Berlin, indeed, Sir Nevile Henderson, the Ambassador, was exhausting the resources of honest diplomacy in maintaining the cause of peace against men who did not desire peace and knew not the meaning of honesty; but at the Privy Council, which the King held on the morning of his arrival in London, it was necessary to make all the preliminary dispositions required for the waging of war. The earliest of nearly three thousand Orders in Council, which would have to be made in the coming years, were now promulgated—legal formalities, previously sanctioned by Parliament, by which a system of regulations was put into force, ranging from the establishment of the blackout to the prohibition of the flying of kites. By such rules, made ever more elaborate and pervasive, the life of the King's subjects would be directed for the next six years—an irksome code enough for a people bred in the tradition of individual freedom, but all knew that they were putting their liberties in pawn in order that liberty itself might have a chance of survival.

As the last week of peace ran out, every crowding phase of the world crisis was instantly communicated to the King. Council after Council was summoned to deal with the intricate formalities of preparation for war. The Prime Minister had long and anxious audiences. Other Ministers whose duties involved them deeply with the dark preoccupations of the time, were received— Lord Halifax, the Foreign Secretary; Lord Chatfield, the Minister for the Co-ordination of Defence. The Queen meanwhile stayed on at Balmoral; there was nothing at the moment for her to do, except pray, as countless thousands of the wives of lesser men were praying, that war might even now be averted. On Sunday, August 27, prayers for peace were offered up on behalf of the whole nation in Westminster Abbey, and the King was there to represent his people in the sight of God, as in that same place he had been consecrated to do two years before. There followed a comparative lull of two days before the pace of the crisis quickened to its final catastrophe.

On Wednesday, August 30, the King devoted most of his day to a tour of the headquarters of the three fighting services, to be shown by the staffs the final preparations for a struggle which, as the expectation then was, might break into tense and violent action from the moment war was declared—or even sooner. In the morning he visited the War Office and the Air Ministry, accompanied by his brother, the Duke of Gloucester, who, with a major-general's commission, was representing the Royal Family in the Army, and by the Duke of Kent, who was serving similarly in the Royal Navy. In the afternoon, the King drove to the Admiralty and was shown the plans of the service in which he had spent his youth, and with which he himself had gone into action in the great battle of Jutland, twenty-three years before.

On September 1, the die was cast. Early in the morning, news reached King and people that German troops had crossed the frontier into Poland, and German aircraft were bombing Warsaw. When the Privy Council met, the King, who had held a number of Councils to order the necessary preparations for war, formally declared that a " state of great emergency " existed; and signed proclamations mobilizing the Navy, calling up the Army and R.A.F. reserves.

All the services were now mobilized, the civilians were prepared for what they must do; and the choice of peace or war lay in Hitler's hands. All the world knew that if the integrity of Poland were violated, Great Britain and France were pledged to come in arms to her assistance.

The King drove to Downing Street for a long talk with his Prime Minister; and while Parliament was summoned to an emergency sitting on Saturday, instructions went to Sir Nevile Henderson to inform the German Government that, failing an assurance by eleven o'clock on Sunday morning that they would withdraw their invading forces, a state of war would exist between Germany and Great Britain. No such assurance came; and accordingly on that Sunday morning the royal declaration of war was brought into force. Within a few days the Governors General, representing the King in each of his Dominions, save Eire, each acting on the advice of his own responsible Ministers, had separately declared war on Germany in the King's name. This was the first time that the Commonwealth had determined the issue of peace and war as a partnership of sovereign states, none able to commit another; but it was shown that the impalpable link of loyalty to the Crown, the only remaining formal bond, was a sufficient guarantee for an overwhelming unity of action. That unity, in which the enemies of the Commonwealth had refused to believe, was to prove their undoing.

It was to all his peoples throughout the world that the King spoke from Buckingham Palace that night, calling them, in the simple emphatic terms that were to become familiar at successive crises of the war, to self-dedication, to courage, labour, and endurance, to faith in the justice of their cause and the Providence that would not allow it to fail. Next day the relentless routine of war descended upon the King, to give him no respite until the very end. Two changes in the outward aspect of his life were immediately apparent to the people. He changed into uniform, wearing in turn the dress of each of the high ranks he bore, an Admiral of the Fleet, a Field-Marshal, a Marshal of the Royal Air Force, and made no further public appearances in mufti; thus he gave visible notice that he considered himself as continuously on duty as any fighting man in his services. Secondly, all references to his future movements disappeared from the public press. This was a new kind of war, against an enemy without scruple and possessing weapons of vast range and hideous potency; none knew when

INSPECTING THE METROPOLITAN POLICE

GREETING AUSTRALIAN TROOPS IN BRITAIN, 1940

the King himself might become a target, and for the sake of security his movements must be concealed. For nearly six years men knew where he had been yesterday, but not where he was today; they were conscious, however, that he was continuously active, and might appear among them when he was least expected, and that awareness, by giving every war worker a sense of being at any moment potentially under a royal eye, played its part in maintaining the national alertness when incalculable issues turned upon it.

That Monday brought the first official visitors of the war to the Palace, the beginning of a stream that was to flow unceasingly. One was Mr. Chamberlain, the other was Lord Gort, already selected to command the Expeditionary Force on the Continent; and with him the King was able to discuss the plans that had been drawn to send his small available army to the assistance of the French in resisting the immediate assault that they expected upon the Maginot Line. For the experience of the old war still governed expectations of the new, and it was not yet revealed to King and commanders-in-chief, any more than to lesser folk, how vastly different was to be the strategy of the coming conflict.

Meanwhile, the Queen had come south from Balmoral, regretfully leaving the two Princesses in the safety of the north. They have grown up so rapidly during the war that it requires an effort of memory to recall that they were then aged only thirteen and ten. As the Queen travelled away from her daughters to London, hundreds of thousands of the children of other mothers were being dispersed from the capital to foster homes in the country; so that in separation, as in so many other of the painful experiences of war, the Royal Family found themselves sharing the common lot. The Queen's first engagement was to accompany the King on a tour of the defence workers of London. The first false air raid warning of the war, which had found the King working at his desk, had called them to the alert at their posts, and the royal party found them still vibrating to the first thrill of excitement, and wondering whether at any moment the reality for which they had been trained might not break with cataclysmic impact upon them.

Now war work was starting in earnest at the Palace; and from henceforth the royal diaries are filled with crowded engagements, all of warlike import—visits to civil defence workers, to war factories, to hospitals (still for the most part standing empty, having been cleared to receive the expected air raid casualties that did not come), to troops, to R.A.F. units, to police stations, to ships of the Royal Navy. As the rhythm of the war gathered power, so did the character of the Royal Family's work alter. The weight of it cannot be appreciated unless there is always

present in the mind's eye something that was scarcely mentioned in the newspapers of the time, and can have but a fleeting reference in a narrative such as this—that austere desk in Buckingham Palace and its counterpart at Windsor. Day after day there was coming to the hands of the King's private secretaries an endless succession of state papers requiring His Majesty's attention. Some would be legal documents, from Acts of Parliament downwards, which needed his signature; others would be papers from the Cabinet or the high command, sent to keep him informed of everything that was done in his name. It was necessary that the King should master the contents of them all, for it was his duty to grasp all the threads of the many-sided war effort of his people, to see the war as a whole, with perhaps wider comprehension because greater detachment than any of his Ministers. It was his kingly function to keep touch with all the bearers

AT A NEW ZEALANDERS' CAMP, 1940

WITH CONTINGENTS FROM CANADA (*ABOVE*) AND RHODESIA (*BELOW*), 1941

of highest responsibility, to be ready at any time to confer with a Cabinet Minister, a commander-in-chief, an ambassador, a distinguished official traveller from an allied country, and send him back to work with mind refreshed and courage strengthened by contact with one who understood the large pattern of the war and the visitor's place in it. To keep abreast of the progress of the war in this way meant several hours of steady desk-work daily—when other engagements interrupted it arrears were apt to mount up alarmingly—and those unrecorded labours have to be constantly borne in mind as the background to all the visible movements of the King among his people.

In the formal words of the Court Circular, which records from day to day, though always in the past tense, the activities of the King and Queen, is to be found the mirror and image of Britain at war. The King's first visits were to his soldiers in training, to the Navy keeping watch in the waste of northern waters beyond Scapa Flow, to the headquarters of Fighter and Coastal Commands of the Royal Air Force. Then came the first heavy blow of the sea war, the loss of H.M.S. *Courageous*; and it must have come home with peculiar poignancy to the King, because this aircraft carrier was one of those proud ships on whose decks he had walked in the sunshine of the August review. Soon afterwards, while he was on a visit to the country, he was brought the news of the sinking of the *Royal Oak*, by one of the most daring German strokes of the war—

IN THE MAGINOT LINE, DECEMBER, 1939

TOUR OF SCOTTISH SHIPYARDS, 1942

another personal grief for a sovereign who can never forget his special ties with the service in which he spent his formative years.

Within the first month of war the King and Queen had contrived to fit in among their multitudinous engagements visits to the headquarters in London of each of the Dominions of the Commonwealth—that is, to the offices of the High Commissioners of Canada, Australia, New

THE GEORGE MEDAL

Zealand and South Africa, as well as of the Indian Empire. Here the King was able to inform himself of the separate programmes of war that each of the sovereign British nations had mapped out for itself—programmes extending the resources of their authors to the utmost, and destined to take on a momentous and saving significance in the, as yet, unimaginable future when the Commonwealth would stand alone, and must so dispose its strength about the globe as to hold the triumphant enemy prisoner in Europe by the tenuous web of sea power.

Meanwhile, behind the grey stone walls and

black railings of the Palace, the King carried on the multifarious business of realm and Empire, turning at frequent intervals from his office work with his secretaries to preside over the necessary formalities of Privy Council meetings, as department after department of Government sought new powers to reinforce the authority of its wartime work. For when Parliament places the liberties of the subject in trust with the executive, as it had done to an unprecedented degree by the Emergency Powers Defence Act, passed at the beginning of the war, the legal form of it is always this, that : " it shall be lawful for His Majesty in Council to make " this, that or the other regulation having the force of law.

To authorize all these regulations, most of them very minute and technical, a few Privy Councillors, generally Ministers and officials, must meet round the King and witness his assent. Another important formality of these early days was the reception of new Ministers, coming to receive their seals of office—most distinguished among them the new First Lord of the Admiralty, Mr. Winston Churchill, who had served the King's father in the same position at the outset of an earlier German war. But interviews like these were seldom allowed to remain on the formal level; the Court Circular, after recording that the right honourable gentleman had been received in audience and kissed hands on appointment, would generally go on to say that he had the honour of being invited to luncheon with Their Majesties ; and the King would discuss the work of the department with his new adviser and store away in his memory a fresh impression of the man and the job.

The King, however, had no intention of conducting a more sedentary war than he could help. He was impatient to go and see for himself the life of his troops in France; for during the months of September and October the British Expeditionary Force of ten divisions had been quietly conveyed across the Channel, undetected apparently by the Luftwaffe and the U-boats, and without the loss of a single ship or man. There had been a little sporadic fighting on the frontier, and the King wished to see what was happening—a demand he has constantly repeated at later stages of the war, when fighting has been hard and anything but sporadic. With the approval of the Cabinet

The King meets and offers his congratulations to a die-caster in an aircraft factory whose prompt action had saved four women workers from being burned to death by molten metal

he crossed the water on December 4, and spent two days inspecting British troops, visiting the forts of the Maginot Line, and gazing over the placid waters of the upper Rhine at the deceptively peaceful German lines beyond. He was received everywhere with enthusiasm, and everywhere he was able to observe the steady resolution of the men, a little puzzled by the strange inactivity to which they seemed to be relegated, but confident in their training and leadership, though under no illusions about the severity of the battle that must sooner or later be joined. The visit was accounted an unqualified success. The King had, of course, been made aware by his Ministers at the beginning that the French Government had entered the war with great reluctance, and that there was grave reason to doubt the wholeheartedness of some of the men in high office. But any misgivings that the royal party may have felt were insufficient to raise any suspicion of the disasters in store; there was nothing to tell the King that it would be four and a half years before he could again see his troops in action on French soil, and that then he would find them, with Americans instead of Frenchmen at their side, struggling desperately to win a first foothold on the Norman shore. He returned to London to receive the news of the first great victory of any of his forces—the defeat of the *Admiral Graf Spee*, by much inferior weight of armament, in the glorious battle of the River Plate.

Soon after the King's return, death took from the Royal Family its oldest member, a link with half-forgotten wars; for in the year when Princess Louise was born, the Duke of Wellington, as Commander-in-chief, was concerned with putting the defence of the country in order against the danger of a French invasion; she had spent her childhood in the days of the Crimean War and the Indian Mutiny, and had married in the last days of the Franco-Prussian War the future Duke of Argyll, with whom she had presided in Queen Victoria's stead over the Dominion of Canada more than half a century ago. The King and Queen, as chief mourners, attended the funeral at Windsor.

That first Christmas of the war the King broadcast to his peoples, his words closing a series of messages from his subjects all round the Empire, in the manner that his father had made

beloved. The hardships and bereavements of war had as yet but lightly touched the members of the British Commonwealth; so unreal indeed did the struggle with Germany superficially appear, in the days when the R.A.F. was still dropping leaflets over Berlin, that popular interest and even partisanship had largely transferred itself to the Russo-Finnish war. The King, advised by his Ministers, of course, knew how deceptive appearances were; the war was flowing in concealed channels, and flowing against the Allies, because Germany was working at full pressure in preparation for the next campaigning season, while in Great Britain the sense of urgent peril had not yet communicated itself to the mass of the people. Twice, during his short Christmas holiday, the King was summoned to London to hold essential Council meetings and give audience to his Ministers. The Christmas broadcast was not an occasion for explicit insistence on the imminence of danger, which would indeed at any time be less a function for the King than for the responsible heads of his Government; but the King's quiet words of greeting and good wishes carried with them an even deeper sense than usual of the vital significance of the world-wide brotherhood to which he spoke, and of the reliance that the world might have to place upon its solidarity in the unknown trials that lay ahead. This broadcast was delivered from the King's study at Sandringham House, which was shortly afterwards closed. Man-power was being steadily drawn away as successive age groups were called up for national service, and the King's households were furnishing their quota like all the rest. Henceforth the Royal Family contented themselves with a country home at Appleton House near by, which had belonged to the King's aunt, Queen Maud of Norway, and which could be managed with a much smaller staff than Sandringham.

The work of the nation was still a continuation of the rearmament that had been in progress at a steadily increasing rate ever since the development of the German menace, rather than a true strategic deployment; and it was this phase of preparation and equipment that the King and Queen went to see when they paid their first visit to war centres in Scotland, in February, 1940. Their tour included ship-building yards, armament factories, the Royal Naval torpedo factory, and A.R.P. organizations in the west of the country. This

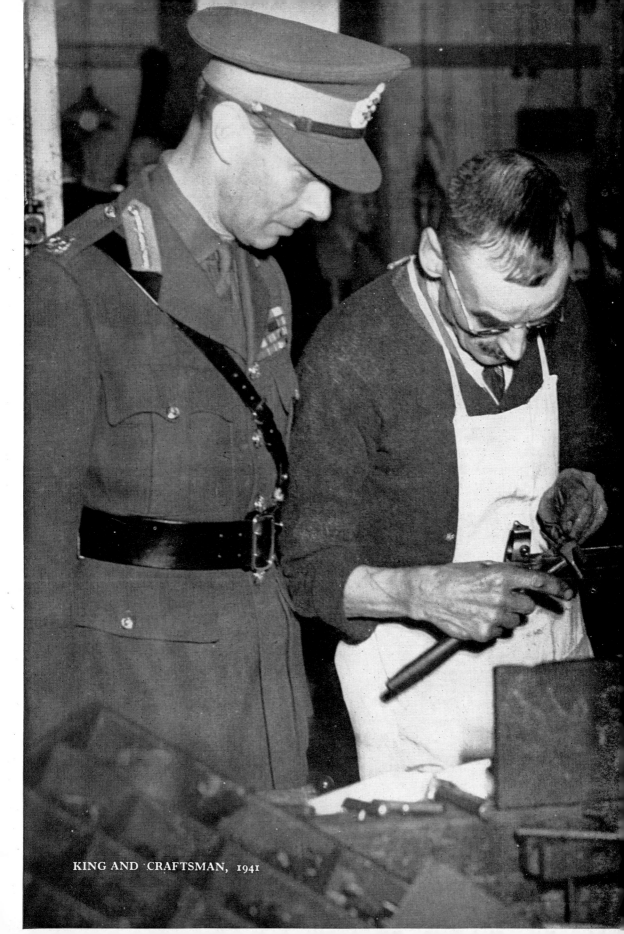

KING AND CRAFTSMAN, 1941

WOMEN'S LAND ARMY, 1942

journey was in a sense the inauguration of the new phase into which the still young reign had passed. It was less than three years since the King and Queen had emerged from the joyous pomp of the Coronation tours, when they had been eagerly awaited everywhere by crowds assembled to do them honour, and there were bands and banquets and fluttering banners wherever they went. Now their way took them through an endless succession of stern and purposeful factories, where there had been no announcement of their coming, and work could scarcely pause for their welcome. But they were moving among the same people whom they had known in so different a mood; each hour had been planned to allow the King and Queen to see every detail of the work that could be crowded into the day, and to allow every possible worker at bench and lathe to see the King and Queen; and to all these men and women the visit of their sovereign doubled the significance of their labour for the nation's cause as surely as their presence had made memorable the gaieties of three years before.

The principal incident of the tour pointed the contrast with the peaceful times that were gone. It was about a year since the Queen, in a blaze of publicity, had launched the country's greatest liner on the Clyde, bestowing her own name upon her—although even then the preoccupations of the darkening European scene had kept the King in London with his Ministers. Now for the second time there was a great launch on the Clyde, not of a liner, but of a man-of-war, the *Duke of York*, a sister ship for the mighty *King George V*; and the King, with Mr. Churchill as First Lord of the Admiralty at his side, sent her down to the water with prayer for the divine blessing upon all who should sail in her to battle. There was no one now to cheer except the men of the shipyard who had worked upon this great new engine of war; there were no rejoicings and no word in the newspapers afterwards, for this was a security secret, and when the King and Queen returned to London, very few, outside the uncommunicative walls of the Admiralty, knew what had been the principal object of their visit to the North. It was an early example of the elaborately contrived secrecy, growing constantly stricter as the conflict became more intense, which was to conceal the movements of the King and Queen, always in advance

and frequently also in retrospect, throughout the war, and which has made it impossible for most of their subjects until now to gain any clear idea of their unceasing activity.

In that interlude of sinister calm, Mr. Sumner Welles, the American Under Secretary of State, was touring Europe on behalf of President Roosevelt, with a mission to report on the realities behind the screen of propaganda that all the belligerents were throwing between themselves and the neutral world. His audience at the Palace was the King's first opportunity since his visit to the United States to meet an American holding high office in Washington. Their conversation was long and frank, and Mr. Welles seems to have found the King's quiet confidence the more impressive by contrast with the strained and rhetorical tone of much to which he had had to listen in other capitals. It was a time when the whole legal framework of American foreign policy was still planned to safeguard the neutrality of the United States in any European quarrel; but the King and the American diplomatist parted equally conscious of a fundamental harmony in their people's outlook on the Nazi menace, and with a sense that before the war was over that harmony was certain, in some way or other, to exercise a momentous influence upon its course.

All this time there was a steady stream of British troops going over to France, as Territorials, militiamen, and others who had been partially trained before war began completed their preparation for active service. In a thinner stream, by now, men who had gone out in the first transports were coming home on leave. These forces, who looked like being the first to be thrown into pitched battle with the enemy, and the seamen who kept the Channel free for them against the lurking menace of the U-boats and the mines, were never out of the King's thoughts. He missed no opportunity of visiting them in camp and barracks to wish them God speed before embarkation; he went down to Dover to inspect the ships and men of the Dover Patrol; and once men on leave who had landed there and were about to entrain for London were astonished to find their King seeking the shortest cut to quick understanding of the harbour and railway routine by himself taking a turn as ticket inspector at Dover Marine station.

Already it was not only an army of the United

Kingdom that was massing to meet the Germans. Secretly and unmolested by the enemy, the First Canadian Division had been brought over to the northern ports during the winter months, and the King went down to Aldershot in January to see the finishing stages of their final training for the front. These, the volunteers from his oldest Dominion, were the first contingent he had yet met from his Empire overseas; and as he walked through the ranks he was struck with the high proportion of men wearing the ribbons of the last war who had returned to the colours to strike another blow at the old enemy. He found time to pause for a word of greeting to nearly all of these veterans. Shortly afterwards there followed another occasion of high imperial interest: the centenary of the annexation of New Zealand. The King and Queen, after sending a birthday message of congratulation to the most remote of their subjects, attended a reception at the Mansion House, where memories of Captain Hobson, who hoisted the Union Jack in the Bay of Islands in January, 1840, were obscured in the mind's eye by another picture, of the armies of New Zealand now mustering under the same flag for service wherever the needs of world war might call them. From this reminder of a world-wide loyalty the King and Queen went on to a tour of aircraft factories in Wales and the West of England, to a further series of military inspections, and to the presentation of new colours to the Irish and Welsh Guards—all interspersed as usual with necessary Councils and audiences and routine business of state. At Easter, as if to defy the enemy to interfere with the picturesque and kindly customs of old England, the King attended Westminster Abbey to distribute, for the first time in person, the Royal Maundy to forty-five old men and forty-five old women—the number corresponding to the years of his age.

These months of the uncertain lull on the Western front served, as the King and Queen continued their tours of munition factories and other war establishments, to evolve a new routine of royal progresses. At a later stage of the war, Field-Marshal Montgomery in his caravan was to make the device of a movable home and office famous; but he had been anticipated by his sovereign. Instead of staying with some nobleman or local magnate, whose house could be made the centre of a tour, as the rulers of England from time immemorial had been accustomed to do, the King and Queen adopted the plan of using the royal train as their mobile headquarters. This arrangement enabled them to dispense with a great deal of customary ceremonial, which in peace helps the people to appreciate the significance of the royal office just as a worthy frame sets off the beauty of a picture, but which becomes a luxury when all available effort is mobilized for war. It also saved time in working through a crowded programme of engagements; and, as domestic staffs of great houses joined the colours or were called up for war employment, it spared many a loyal subject the embarrassment of having to entertain his sovereign with cramped resources. The system was maintained throughout the war, during which the King travelled well over half a million miles in this way—a remarkable testimony to the solid workmanship of the men who had built the train for Queen Victoria, though she did not live to use it. This great distance, the equivalent of twenty times the circumference of the globe at the equator, has to be added to the thousands of miles of the King's wartime journeys by air and sea on his visits to his forces abroad.

One formality that the King ordered to be suspended until after the war was the ceremonial meeting of the Sovereign by his personal representative, the Lord Lieutenant, in each county that he visited. It was to see the people at war that the King and Queen travelled, and it was for the representatives of the war service of the people—the regional commissioners, the naval, military, and air force commanders—to meet the royal party at the stations and conduct them on their tours. But however far they went there was no remission of the royal work in the capital. Wherever they halted for the night, generally choosing some quiet siding from which the King and Queen could take a stroll after dinner, undisturbed by crowds, their train was connected up to the national telephone system, to enable the King to keep in touch with his private secretaries at Buckingham Palace, and through them with his Ministers. When air raids began to be threatening, the railway companies took care to provide a specially-built shelter at each night's stopping place. Among the first entries on the itinerary of the royal train are Wolverhampton, Birmingham, South Lancashire, Dorset; but to transcribe the whole list would be to compile

THE ROYAL FAMILY AT HOME

WITH SURVIVORS OF DUNKIRK

an abbreviated gazetteer of Great Britain and Northern Ireland.

With Hitler's treacherous onslaught upon Norway and Denmark on April 9, 1940, the storm clouds, which had been piling up for so long, burst over Europe in the fury of the blitzkrieg, and the British war effort, hitherto lethargic if measured by later standards, was swept into a sudden crescendo. The King gave his authority for an expedition to the relief of his new allies; and in the secret war room at the Admiralty, guided by Mr. Churchill, he followed on the charts, with the informed interest of a trained naval officer, the progress of a great naval battle off the Norwegian coast, as the wireless messages came in and were decoded. Intervention, however, was too late to overtake the start the enemy had seized; the expedition had to be withdrawn, and in the stormy political sequel the Government fell. On May 10, the day after the King had signed the proclamation calling up men for service up to the age of thirty-six, Mr. Neville Chamberlain sought an audience in order to tender his resignation; and the King, whose function it is, on these occasions, to give expression to the evident desire of Parliament and people, had no hesitation in calling on Mr. Winston Churchill to form a new administration. Much controversy besets the policy of Neville Chamberlain in his later years; but the King knew him as a loyal servant, and a Prime Minister who had laboured devotedly in the cause of peace. It is understood that he offered, on his retirement, to advance him to high rank in the peerage; but Mr. Chamberlain asked leave, like his father before him, to remain in the House of Commons to the last, and with characteristic absence of rancour accepted the office of Lord President of the Council under his former subordinate. For the next few days the King was occupied in receiving the outgoing Ministers, who came to surrender their seals of office, and in installing their successors, the men who had accepted Mr. Churchill's invitation to share with him " blood, toil, tears and sweat."

Just as the new Government was taking office the full fury of the armed multitudes of Germany burst, in all their immense superiority of armament, over the boundaries of the Netherlands, Belgium, and France. If there is any life or reality in the conception of representative monarchy that has been expressed in these pages, those days

of unimagined disaster must have fallen with peculiar and terrible impact upon the King. It was his troops, the men whom he had met and known and in whose devotion he had taken such pride, that were now being borne backwards by overwhelming numbers towards Dunkirk; it was his duty to share, and he did share, in the anxieties of all their kindred at home and the sorrows of the bereaved; and he could not be shielded, as most of us were, by a merciful ignorance of the real desperateness of the situation. In the midst of the distresses of his own country he was called upon to befriend those who had suffered even greater calamity. It is an ancient and honourable English tradition to give sanctuary to rulers and statesmen who have been driven out of their own lands; many of King George's ancestors have welcomed foreign princes since the future King Louis IV took refuge at the court of King Athelstan, more than a thousand years ago. But now England was to become on an unexampled scale an ark of salvation in which patriots of many lands could ride out the storm until the German inundation should subside, and where they could lay their plans for the reconstruction of a desolated world. The King's meetings with these illustrious exiles punctuate the calendar of his harassed days while Western Europe was going down before the advancing flood. The first to arrive was the brave Queen Wilhelmina of the Netherlands, rescued by the Royal Navy and seeking in England not so much a refuge as a vantage-point from which she could continue to direct and inspire the heroic resistance of her subjects in the lands that had been overwhelmed. The King went to Liverpool Street Station, passed through the crowds of London office workers homeward bound after the day's work, and amid their cheers welcomed his sister sovereign on the platform.

Meanwhile, he was paying frequent visits to the War Office to meet the military chiefs and study on the large-scale maps the ominous development of the strategic situation, while the Prime Minister and the Chief of the Imperial General Staff, Sir Edmund Ironside, visited him at the Palace to explain the growing threat to the British Expeditionary Force. On Empire Day he broadcast a message to his peoples, in a tone of sombre resolution; and on Sunday, May 26, he called the nation to prayer, and as their head and

REVIEW OF THE FREE FRENCH IN BRITAIN, WITH GENERAL DE GAULLE, 1940

chief representative himself attended, with the Queen, at Westminster Abbey. But there were still heavier blows to come. On May 28, the King learnt that King Leopold of the Belgians, with his army, had surrendered to the enemy, and that only headlong retreat could save the British Expeditionary Force from being surrounded and completely cut off from all communication with England.

Even at this crisis the ordinary work of government had to go on, and the King found time to visit R.A.F. units in various parts of the country and to decorate some of the first airmen who had been recommended for distinguished service. But all the while he was keeping in hourly touch with his Ministers, and facing the dreadful knowledge that his army in France was about to undertake the perilous enterprise of an embarkation under the fire of an enemy possessing overwhelming superiority by land and air, and that his best strategic advisers believed that not more than a tenth of them could expect to escape. He had

no other army sufficiently trained and armed to take the field; and what was to become of himself and his country after these gallant divisions were overwhelmed no man dared prophesy.

Owing to the superb endurance and co-operation of all three services, with the help of many amateur seamen who rose to the occasion with the daring and resource of a great maritime tradition, the full catastrophe that had been feared was triumphantly evaded. But the plight of the country was only partly relieved, for its whole heavy armament had been lost, and the German hordes were still sweeping on across a France that was manifestly incapable of defending itself.

The King had followed every detail of the great retreat and evacuation as the telegrams came in from Lord Gort's headquarters; among them was one to say that his brother, the Duke of Gloucester, who was serving as Chief Liaison Officer to the Commander-in-Chief, had been wounded at Arras. Happily the wound was slight. On June 3, the "Operation Dynamo" was complete; more than 300,000 men had been rescued from Dunkirk where it was feared that not more than 30,000 could escape; and on June 5, three British Lieutenant-Generals, Brooke, Adam, and Lindsell, accompanied by the French Admiral Abrial, came to Buckingham Palace to give the King a first-hand account of the retreat, the battle, and the deliverance. Having heard the experiences of the high officers, the King decided immediately to go and see the rank and file of the survivors. The very next day, accompanied by the Duke of Gloucester, he was off to Aldershot to inspect one of the returned divisions, one that he had visited only a few months ago and found at full strength and eager for battle. It was eager for battle still, only too anxious indeed for an opportunity of revenge upon the victorious enemy. But shorn of its guns and transport, with scarcely a rifle between a dozen men, it was in no condition to return to the field, though officers and men bore themselves as proudly on parade before the King as if it had been a peace-time review—as indeed they had every right and reason to do. The following weeks saw many more royal visits to mangled divisions and battered regiments, as the tragically small and ill-armed remnant of the British Expeditionary Force struggled to gather itself together again into the semblance of a fighting army. Field-Marshal Alexander, then at the head of the southern or invasion command, has recorded his testimony to the effect of the King's visits in restoring the men's confidence in themselves, for his calm presence, his upright soldierly bearing, and his evident pride in and reliance upon them put fresh heart into the exhausted troops.

But for all the gallant effort at recovery, it was clear that a restored British army would be too late to intervene again in the Battle of France.

NORWEGIAN SAILORS PARADE AT PLYMOUTH, 1941

TOUR OF R.A.F. FIGHTER STATIONS, 1942

While they were closing the diminished ranks Mr. Churchill was a constant visitor to the Palace, his face grave and set as he brought ever more grievous tidings of the desperate plight of the ally across the Channel. He obtained the King's consent to the romantic and chivalrous offer of a united citizenship and a common government with France. Little was said at the time of the personal sacrifice made by the King in extending this invitation; but a little thought will show that he was putting his own throne in jeopardy, for no man could foretell what ultimate consequences might flow from the organic union between an ancient monarchy and a republic already prostrate under the heel of its implacable enemies. The King, however, in the hour when his subjects were throwing all they had, and were, into the common stock, did not hesitate to risk everything ; it was the consummation of the famous Entente in the making of which a generation earlier his grandfather, Edward VII, had played a leading part; and now, in the hour of adversity, he honoured the ancestral obligation with unquestioning fullness of generosity. The offer went unheeded by the craven rulers who had already usurped the name of the Government of France; and in a little while the French forces laid down their arms. In that darkest hour of French history some comfort was brought to the stricken people by the moving broadcast in which the Queen of England, speaking in their own language to the women of France, exhorted them to courage and patience in the years of oppression and suffering on which they were about to enter, and by her faith that their country would rise on stepping-stones of its dead self to the level of its historic greatness. Resurgent France has justified the Queen's confidence; and we know from the testimony of many witnesses that the memory of that broadcast helped to strengthen the spirit of resistance in many French hearts during the years of occupation.

The fall of France caused another Government to seek refuge in England—that of Poland, which had been established in Paris since their own country was overrun. There was little enough of visible security to offer them, for the island was under immediate threat of invasion, and Marshal Pétain had just declared that England would, in a few weeks, have its neck wrung like a chicken. Mr. Churchill's comment on that rash prophecy is sufficiently well known. There was no trace, however, of the precariousness of the situation on the King's face when he went to Paddington to meet the Polish President and Cabinet; and by greeting them with his usual unruffled courtesy he gave them their first clear impression of the staunchness of the people among whom henceforth their lot was to be cast, and who would stand or fall with the cause of European freedom.

With the Sovereigns, Presidents and other heads of states—such as General de Gaulle, leader of the Fighting French—who came to Great Britain from the invaded countries, and with their Ministers, the King maintained relations, after the first warmth of greeting, on the same correct diplomatic footing as when they were in their own lands. It was the right course; this was not an occasion for informality. Some of these persecuted statesmen had been hunted over half a continent; others had risked everything in repudiating the pusillanimous counsel of colleagues who had submitted to the enemy; and to maintain the punctilio of diplomatic intercourse was to help them to realize that there was still stability in the world and still recognition of the dignity of free men, even in exile. So British ambassadors and ministers were appointed to the foreign courts, and given their letters of credence from the King as His Majesty's Envoys Extraordinary and Ministers Plenipotentiary, just as if they were taking up residence in the British Embassy at Oslo or the Hague, or, later on, Belgrade; and the representatives of the exiled governments came to Buckingham Palace to present their credentials to the King in the same way, even though the two ambassadors, exchanged between the British and a foreign court, might be living in adjoining streets in London and meeting constantly in one of the clubs frequented by diplomats. Pomp and circumstance can be a very present help in time of trouble.

King Haakon of Norway, whose late Queen was a sister of King George V, was, with his son, Crown Prince Olaf, the most frequent of the royal visitors to Buckingham Palace; indeed, to the end of the war he used to call regularly for his personal mail, which was addressed there in order to keep the secret of his actual residence. During the absence of Lord Athlone and Princess Alice, representing the King in his Dominion of Canada, their Sussex home at Balcombe was, for a long time, occupied by the Queen of the Netherlands. King George of the Hellenes and King Peter of Yugoslavia were often guests of the Royal Family at luncheon—always a simple meal of three courses in strict conformity with the rationing regulations. But as a general rule the lives of the foreign courts were conducted as separately from that of "the Court of St. James's" as if they were divided by the normal distances and frontiers. By every graceful observance of courtesy they were shown that they were regarded as the headquarters of sovereign states.

These distinguished visitors settled into their wartime homes well knowing that their hosts, with the best will in the world, could not guarantee them any security of tenure. For now, in July, 1940, the threat of invasion was looming in its most formidable proportions. In order to land an army of irresistible strength the enemy needed only command of the air over southern England; and the world, reckoning up the immense superiority of the Luftwaffe over the R.A.F., concluded that he could win that command when he liked. Only the British, who relied less on arithmetic, refused to acknowledge the necessary result of the calculation, and went on with their plans of resistance as if they expected their island to remain their own. The King went down to Dover to inspect the meagre defences, prepared on the assumption of a friendly shore on the other side of the Straits; he spent the day talking to the local defence commanders, examining their tank traps, beach minefields, wire entanglements and the like, and found, as he expected, that the temper of the men was as staunch as the fortifications were vulnerable. Work was going forward with unresting speed to strengthen them, and if only a little time could be won for their completion the white walls of Old England, which had stood unchallenged for so many centuries, might yet be rendered impregnable against the terrible engines of modern assault. Having satisfied himself that everything possible was being done to meet the expected attack, the King returned to London, and next day was holding an investiture as usual at the Palace. Nothing in the whole war was allowed to interrupt the simple ritual of these ceremonies; they continued through the days of imminent invasion, through the dark winter of the great air raids, sometimes while the enemy was actually over London, until the heroes of the

EARLY DAYS (1940) OF THE L.D.V., AFTERWARDS THE HOME GUARD

THE PRINCESS ROYAL VISITS A MIXED A.A. BATTERY IN SCOTLAND

early defensive battles were gradually replaced by the victors of Africa and Italy, of France and the Low Countries, finally by the conquerors of Germany itself, coming to receive the honours and rewards of their gallant service.

Frequent councils were now being held, to translate into formal shape the secret preparations that were being made to meet the emergency of invasion. The Prime Minister and the Lord President, with Mr. Eden as Secretary of State for War, were in constant attendance at the Palace. Among an immense mass of administrative business arising out of the new Act that summoned the whole people to put themselves and their property " at the disposal of His Majesty," plans had to be made for the removal of Parliament, the great departments of state, and the royal residence, in case London should fall into the enemy's power or be closely threatened. Since the defeat of Germany it has been revealed that the alternative seat of government was to have been Shakespeare's town of Stratford on Avon, the very heart of England. Besides taking part in these official schemes for the evacuation of the

capital, the King, with the Queen, had to make a very delicate decision, which was personal to themselves. Many of their subjects of all ranks were now hastening to send away their children to safe harbourage in hospitable America, or in the British Dominions across the seas, where they might grow up in freedom though the British Isles might suffer the horrors of a German occupation. The royal family, however, decided that such relief from anxiety was not for them. Their exalted station had its own inescapable obligations of honour; and the two princesses, although they were kept out of London during the air raids, like children of less eminent rank, remained to share the dangers of the country that one of them will some day rule.

In that perilous summer the list of royal inspections tended to be concentrated upon the Air Force, as was natural, seeing that to the airmen the main burden of the war was for the time being transferred. The King visited Kenley, Northolt, and other fighter stations of the famous Number Eleven Group, and met his young fighter pilots, the immortal "few" of the Battle of Britain, just as they came down to snatch a brief rest from the incessant combats, fought at six miles a minute and generally against all but impossible odds. Exhausted as they were by their heroic efforts, they were proud of the opportunity to tell their Sovereign something of the epic fight that was being fought in his service. From the airfields he went on to visit troops training in earnest haste, in order to master the new lessons taught by the experience of the Battle of France in time to put them into practice in the expected campaign on British ground; and to the munition factories, now working in shifts all round the clock to produce ammunition for the guns of the defence and replace the multifarious equipment that had been lost at Dunkirk.

Meanwhile, a new army had sprung from the soil to serve the King—the Local Defence Volunteers, without uniforms and almost without weapons, but resolute in defiance, with a spirit that guaranteed that the manhood of England, young and old, would lay down their lives even in hopeless combat before the enemy was master of the land. The King went at once to see a contingent of them, and spent Saturday watching their strenuous exercises. Within a month they had transformed themselves into an effective fighting instrument, and on the advice of the Prime Minister the King had bestowed upon them the finer title of the Home Guard. The armed citizens marched past him, several thousand strong, at a formal review at West Wickham, and he had evidence that already an invading army would find the English countryside vastly more difficult to penetrate than it had been at the moment of the fall of France. He had given active

QUEEN MARY WATCHES A.A. GUNNERS AT DRILL

encouragement to the formation of Home Guard companies at both Buckingham Palace and Windsor Castle, and himself took part in some of their training. Even the Queen and other royal ladies learned to use a rifle and a revolver; for in those days of parachute descents from the clouds, as had been shown on the Continent, no one in the land could feel secure against the possibility of being unexpectedly confronted with an armed German. Indeed, there was a time when the advisers of the Crown had to take seriously into account the legal complications that would follow if the King were ambushed and carried off as a prisoner of war.

The war, as the King's advisers well knew, must soon pass from the phase of air battles by daylight to mass attack upon industrial and probably civilian objectives. Defence resources were being hurriedly concentrated to meet the assault. The London docks, for instance, would certainly be an early target, and strong forces were on guard there day and night. The King took the first opportunity to go to the docks, talk to the men, study their duties and examine their arms. The threat was, of course, no less immediate to the bases of sea power; and the King accordingly travelled all over the threatened South of England to visit the ships, shore establishments and air stations of the Royal Navy. On these journeys, though as usual he travelled without military escort, the King now took the precaution of exchanging his ordinary saloon car for one that had been made bullet-proof and splinter-proof. He conformed also to the orders issued to the men of all the Services, of which he was the head, and invariably carried his steel helmet—but very rarely put it on—and his service respirator.

The increase of pressure that summer was perhaps more severe upon women than on men, since they had hitherto been less intensively mobilized; so, after the King had toured the coast defences and armament factories in the North Midlands, he took the Queen with him to see the concentrated work that was being done in the aircraft factories in the south. Here were being built, in a stern contest with time, the night fighters that would be required to defend the civil population in the coming winter. As autumn drew on, the King found time to make himself acquainted with another vital aspect of national preparation by visiting a holiday camp where schoolboys were living while they helped to bring in the harvest. Among them he was to be seen sitting in the open air eating his lunch in the shade of a haystack—a pleasant interlude for Sovereign and subjects alike in the rather grim routine of these inspections. He did not neglect the foreign contingents who were helping with the preparations for the defence of his country, visiting, for instance, Polish airmen quartered in the Midlands and the training camp in the south where the military forces of the Free French were gathering to resume the fight under General de Gaulle.

The second year of the war began dramatically for the King, who held an investiture at Buckingham Palace during an air raid on September 3— the first time British subjects had been decorated by their King under bombardment from the sky. The end of that week was the beginning of the intensive night attack upon London. On September 9 Mr. Morrison came to the Palace in his capacity as Minister of Home Security, and told the King of the distress in the East End after several severe attacks in which many homes had been destroyed and heavy casualties inflicted. The King immediately replied that he would go in person to the affected areas, and he set off immediately, with little formality and only the shortest and most scanty preparation, on the first of many scores of visits to scenes of devastation that he and the Queen were to make together or separately. In so doing they were following the natural instincts of compassion for their suffering people, and certainly had no thought of the incalculable effect their gesture would have upon nations across the ocean; but there is no doubt that these visits of sympathy had decisive consequence in raising the popularity and prestige of the King and Queen to the highest level in the United States and all over the free world. In their visits to factories and munition works they had been following, though with a reduced formality consonant with the changed times, the practice of King George V and Queen Mary in the last war. But by going directly, as he so often did, to the scene of raid damage and walking through the debris in the streets where unexploded bombs and land-mines might still be concealed, the King—at the cost of the peace of mind of the officials who were responsible for his

THE KING AND THE DUKE OF KENT GREET MR. WINANT, U.S. AMBASSADOR, 1941

safety—was now setting a new standard of monarchy. This, after all, was the work of the supreme representative; his people had been struck by the enemy, their homes wrecked and their dear ones killed; and the King saw it as his paramount duty to be immediately among them, bringing the assurance that the whole of their countrymen, for whom he alone could speak, were with them in sympathy.

On that first visit to the bombed-out victims in the East End nothing in the King's manner conveyed any hint of his knowledge that at that moment a time bomb weighing 250 pounds was lying in his own home at Buckingham Palace and might explode at any moment. It did, in fact, explode the next day, when the King and Queen were at Windsor, wrecking the swimming pool which had been built for the Princesses two years before, breaking windows in the King's and Queen's bedrooms, and doing other damage. Thus, from the very start, the King and Queen shared with their subjects the hardship of having their homes damaged by wanton bombs from the air. As Mr. Morrison, the Home Secretary, said, this bombing of Buckingham Palace was a blunder of the first order and had the effect, not of harming the Royal Family, but of increasing the affection of the people for the King and Queen who shared their perils.

The Palace was bombed again the same week; and this time the King and Queen were in residence. At about 11 o'clock, on September 13, they looked out of the windows and saw the bombs drop. Five in all fell on and about the Palace, smashing a hundred windows, wrecking the Chapel, and filling the passages with tons of debris. Although many valuable church ornaments were lost, Queen Victoria's family bible, in which all royal births are recorded, was recovered from the wreckage. On this occasion there were, unhappily, some casualties, three plumbers at work in the south wing of the Palace being injured, one of them fatally. The King and Queen made an immediate tour of the damaged parts, talking to shaken members of the staff, and leaving afterwards for another visit to East London, where they appeared quite unmoved by their narrow escape. Two days later another bomb crashed, without exploding, through the roof and the Queen's apartments to the ground floor.

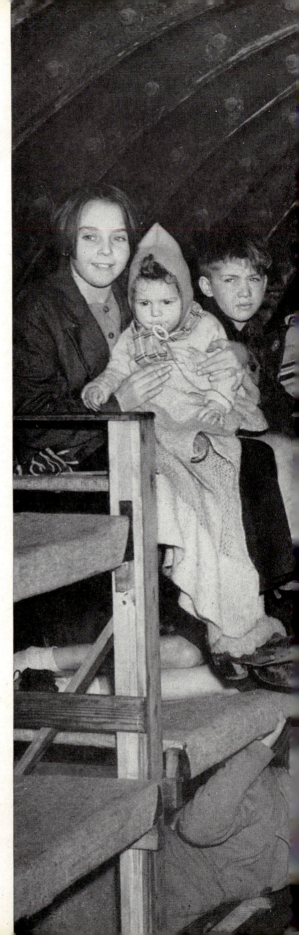

Altogether, Buckingham Palace was bombed nine times during the war, suffering in the last year from both flying bombs and rockets. These repeated attacks on their own home enabled the King and Queen to speak with real understanding to the sufferers whom they met on their numerous visits to the bombed streets of London and other towns throughout the land.

It was an astonishing experience to accompany the King and Queen on one of these expeditions and to see the new representative monarchy in action. Travelling in an ordinary-looking saloon car with military number plate and splinter-proof windows, the King and Queen had none of the customary amenities of open roads, cleared in advance for a royal progress; instead, a police motor cyclist rode ahead, charged with the difficult and sometimes impossible task of clearing busy London traffic only a few seconds before the royal car approached. Then came a police car, the royal car, and perhaps a third containing the staff; no more. This little procession became familiar to Londoners. They would stand cheering at Westminster Bridge, the Marble Arch and other focal points as the cars sped by. Although the police cyclist would thrust his way unceremoniously into the traffic blocks when the King was held up on his own highway, and marshal lorries and carts, buses and military cars, this way and that until the road was clear, there were never any advance instructions; and when the King and Queen reached the bombed area, as often as not wardens and rescue workers had no inkling that they were expected. If that was the case it was as the King desired.

London is divided into four police districts, and it was the duty of the Deputy Assistant Commissioner in charge of each district in turn to accompany the King and Queen through the streets of his domain, and take the anxious responsibility for their safety. In addition, regular police officers were attached to them and accompanied them everywhere. But once the King and Queen left their car, the police and every one else were powerless. Crowds of men and women, still dazed by the bombs, thronged about them, swallowed them up, separated them from their staff, and took them to their hearts. Nothing like the warmth of these receptions in hours of tragic disaster has been seen before or since. The King, in Field-Marshal's uniform, would take his stand

on some uneasy vantage point of balanced rubble and listen to the story the senior warden told about the "incident"—to use the curiously colourless term that official jargon devised to cover every variety of catastrophic destruction. The Queen would walk gravely and quietly among the homeless, talking with gentle understanding to men and women, and giving them, by her mere presence and her delicately expressed sympathy, the encouragement and impulse they needed to pick up the broken threads of life. Over and over again, people from the poorest homes, the whole of whose meagre possessions had dissolved a few hours before into the dreadful grey dust that in those days pervaded the air of London, stood in the smoking ruins of their homes and cried in broken voices: "God bless you—God bless you both." Never can any monarch have received tributes more moving and sincere; and never, certainly, have King and people felt themselves more completely as one.

Photographs taken of these incidents—a small selection of which illustrates these pages—show the King and Queen engulfed in a swarm of men and women with no visible protection round them. But, though equerries and ladies in waiting, police chiefs and regional commissioners might be irresistibly swept aside, about the King and Queen there was always a little space left. The good manners of the Londoner are instinctive and famous; and the King and Queen always had room to move.

They went into the extemporized rest centres for the homeless and talked to bed-ridden victims of shock, to old men and women too feeble to move; and everywhere and all the time, and most of all where suffering was most grievous, they were impressed by the unfailing cheerfulness of the people. Perhaps they themselves did not know, but their subjects will not easily forget, how much they contributed to keep up the spirits of the victims.

The fighting spirit of the people was indeed always apparent in the midst of these scenes of suffering. The cry was never "put a stop to this" but always "give it back to them." No one knew better than the King that it would some day be given back to them, but also how impossible it was to give it now. He understood the terrifying weakness of the R.A.F. in those days; he was also fully informed of the gigantic future plans

IN BERMONDSEY, A MUCH-BOMBED LONDON BOROUGH, 1941

THE WRECKED CATHEDRAL, COVENTRY, 1940

VISITING BRITAIN'S BOMBED TOWNS—PLYMOUTH

LEAVING A BADLY DAMAGED HOME AT HULL, 1940

for the bombing of Germany at a later date. He must have been tempted, when he heard those cries for retaliation, to give some sign of encouragement or hope; and many may perhaps have wondered why he never did. Apart from considerations of security, there was another reason. The King is a strictly constitutional sovereign; he can act only on the advice of his Ministers, and where questions of policy are even remotely involved, he is absolutely scrupulous to make no reference in public to future actions.

News of the bombing of Coventry, when the German brutality which had destroyed Warsaw and Rotterdam was exhibited for the first time against a comparatively small British city, reached the King one evening in the country. Appreciating at once that this was something new in atrocities, he sent a message to Mr. Herbert Morrison that he would drive to Coventry early in the morning. He reached the city while shaken walls were still falling. Many months later, when the Queen visited Coventry to inspect the plans

for rebuilding, the King heard that over a hundred live parachute mines had been found among the ruins through which he had walked. Danger, indeed, surrounded him many times on these visits of sympathy. They continued throughout that grim winter; as town after town—Southampton, Hull, Birmingham, Bristol, Liverpool, Sheffield, Plymouth, Portsmouth—became the target of the German attack, the King, and usually the Queen with him, hastened to place himself among his suffering subjects. But none of these later visits was quite so spontaneously informal as that first dramatic dash to Coventry; and the picture of the King, stunned like all who were there at the immensity of the destruction, picking his way with the Lord Mayor and the heads of the Civil Defence Services between mounds of smashed glass and pulverized bricks, deserves a place in any history of Great Britain at war.

In London, meanwhile, the King and Queen made repeated tours of the air raid shelters. They

THROUGH THE DAMAGED STREETS OF BATH, 1942

SHEFFIELD, 1940

had a number of talks with the tube dwellers, and became thoroughly acquainted with the strange communal life which was growing up underground. Much of it was pitiful; but none of it was self-pitying, and, indeed, here as everywhere else the unfailing resolution and high spirits of the people made the new social life always contented and sometimes uproariously cheerful. In such apparently unfavourable homes as the Stepney deep shelter or the disused Lambeth tube station, the King and Queen were shown that London life was still very much itself and that they were regarded by the people as an essential part of it.

They themselves never had to use the special shelters provided for them wherever their train stopped for the night. But their own shelter at the Palace—a big underground room fitted with telephones and equipment to enable the King to work through the raids—was needed several times, both during the early blitz and during the flying bomb attacks at the end of the war. On one memorable occasion, however, when Buckingham Palace was itself bombed in daylight, the King and Queen were far from shelter, and there were moments of extreme anxiety for all their staff after the explosion before it was known that they were unhurt.

The passive resistance of civilians, however, was only one-half of the air war that was raging; the King and Queen were simultaneously following the active side of its progress. On the night before the great opening bombardment of the London Docks, they were together in the secret headquarters of Fighter Command at Stanmore and talked to the A.O.C., the present Lord Dowding, and his staff who were directing the defensive battle. Later, at the Air Ministry, Sir Charles Portal, Chief of the Air Staff, gave the King an authoritative survey of the whole scope of the air war as it then was, and as the R.A.F. expected it to develop. The King also went to the headquarters of Coastal Command and to many R.A.F. stations in the country, where he could meet the pilots and crews who were actually carrying out the plans that had been explained to him at the higher levels of command. His tours included the A.A. units in the London Defence Zone; and once he spent a night at a station of Bomber Command, where he could see the twin-engined bombers, the largest he then possessed, going and coming from the first small raids on the enemy—the tentative beginnings of a campaign which would reach its consummation years later, when the giant Lancasters went out to shatter the fortifications of the Atlantic Wall and blast the war industries of the enemy out of existence.

As the campaign developed, the King continued to follow every move; and gradually he saw the offensive phase gaining upon, and at last totally displacing, the defensive. As early as May, 1941, he saw the first British parachute troops practising their fantastically novel tactics.

The culmination of all that the King and Queen saw of the air war was reached in the autumn of 1944 when they visited the gunners of A.A. Command, under General Sir Frederick Pile, and saw them fight the flying bombs. In the open fields of Surrey they sat among the 4·5 guns, saw the men and girls run out as the radar signals came through, and watched the gunners engage eight targets in succession. That day, unhappily, there was only one kill; but that was an interesting example of co-operation between the defensive forces in the air and on the ground. The bomb was hit by A.A. shells, and finished off in full view of the King and Queen by a fast-flying Tempest fighter. The King and Queen had been shown a remarkable example of the immense advance in mastery of the air that had been made since those early days of almost desperate struggle in 1940. It was, though no one knew it then, the last time that the King would move among men and women of his Forces while they were engaged in battle at home.

☆   ☆   ☆

IN the foregoing pages there have been occasional references to investitures. These ceremonies have taken so large a place in the King's wartime life that it is worth while to pause and consider them. By immemorial tradition, the King is the

VISIT TO SCOTLAND—AN ENGINEERING WORKS, 1943

BIRMINGHAM (*ABOVE*), 1942, AND SWANSEA (*BELOW*), 1941

Fountain of Honour. In this, as in all else, he acts as the representative of his people, rewarding those who have served the people valiantly and faithfully, and decorating them, that the people may recognize those who have deserved well of them. Throughout the war the King has treated this as one of his most important functions; and in honouring the service of his fighting men he has introduced new features into ancient ceremonial, and studied to bring Buckingham Palace into closer touch with the life of the nation.

Over 32,000 men and women were personally decorated by the King at Buckingham Palace between 1940 and the early months of 1945. Each of these was allowed to bring two relations or friends to watch the ceremony, so that nearly 100,000 of the King's subjects, most of whom were entering the Palace gates for the first time, saw him in his home.

The full ceremonial associated with investiture during the war grew up gradually. It was held in the stately red-carpeted Grand Hall of the Palace, hung with portraits of former Kings and Queens. Here, under the soft lights used to tone down what might otherwise be the harsh effect of the prevailing crimson, was erected a long dais, also covered in red, looking rather like a ship's poop. The Yeomen of the Guard in the scarlet and gold of their late seventeenth-century uniform were posted round the Chamber, in curious contrast with minor Palace officials who, as members of the Home Guard, appeared at the investitures in khaki battledress. Thus the senior and the junior branches of the land forces of the Crown were on duty together.

Although it had hitherto been primarily the privilege of officers to receive their decorations from the Sovereign's own hand, the King announced, early in 1940, that he intended to decorate personally N.C.O.s of all the services who won medals for gallantry; and he afterwards extended the privilege to all ranks, to the women's services, and to the winners of civilian awards for valour. A further extension of the older practices was made at the King's personal wish, when the next of kin of those killed in action or dying on active service were brought to the Palace to receive the medals or decorations they had won. By these successive enlargements of the old routine the King voluntarily imposed upon himself an immense new labour, to which the only compulsion was his own desire to honour those who had served the nation in his name. He was, indeed, reflecting or anticipating the movement of public opinion, as he did also in September, 1940, when he met the general wish for some special recognition of civilian gallantry in the air raids by the institution of the George Cross —a decoration intended to have and to convey prestige similar to that of the Victoria Cross—and its more widely distributed subsidiary, the George Medal. Two years later, when he bestowed the George Cross upon the unconquerable island of Malta, he again exactly interpreted and crystallized public feeling.

Soon afterwards the King used a similar gesture as a means of expressing his admiration and that of his people for their stalwart Russian ally, with whose fighting men, to his great regret, he never had the opportunity to make personal contact, as he had done with the Americans and with all the exiled armies and navies that had made the British Isles their base. On February 21, 1943, when the free world was applauding the triumph of the long-suffering heroic citizens of Stalingrad, he sent a telegram to the head of the Russian state, M. Kalinin, the Chairman of the Presidium of the Supreme Soviet Council, informing him of his intention to bestow a Sword of Honour on the victorious city. Nine months later Mr. Churchill was in Moscow to confer with Marshal Stalin, and in the afternoon of November 29, 1943, solemnly presented the King's gift. Marshal Stalin kissed the sword when he took it ; and observers declared that even that man of steel was visibly moved. Symbolic Red Stars gleamed in the scabbard and on the hilt of the sword, which was a full-sized, two-handed fighting weapon, with a double-edged blade forged of finest English steel by a veteran craftsman. Along its blade ran the King's inscription: " To the steel-hearted citizens of Stalingrad, the gift of King George VI in token of the homage of the British people." On February 2, 1944, anniversary of the surrender of the Sixth German Army at the city, the sword was handed over by Marshal Budyenny to the keeping of Stalingrad.

Several investitures were cancelled during the months of attack by flying bombs, and some of the Birthday Honours of 1944 were actually conferred in the royal air raid shelter underneath the Palace. One of the notable functions of that

AT A RECEPTION CENTRE FOR THE HOMELESS ON MERSEYSIDE, 1940

IN SOUTHAMPTON, 1940

year had been a presentation of medals held at eleven o'clock on the morning of June 6, when the first news of the landings in Normandy was just coming in.

There was originally a technical distinction between investitures and presentations of medals, which was based upon a principle that gave less weight to the nature of the award than to the rank of the recipient. The opposite principle, which is certainly nearer to the hearts of the people at the present day, was gaining upon it all through the war, and tended to break down the old distinctions. The King entirely sympathized with this tendency, and assisted it in many ways. A V.C., for instance, however humble his rank, took precedence of every one else at investitures; and by the King's command the string band of the Guards Regiment on duty, which normally played throughout the proceedings, ceased playing while the Lord Chamberlain read out the citation for V.C.s, and G.C.s. In 1942, soon after he had ordered that the Merchant Navy should be made eligible for the D.S.O., C.G.M. and D.S.M. on the same terms as the Royal Navy, the King made another innovation which was greatly appreciated in the Fleet. Henceforth, officers and men from one ship who had won decorations together came to the Palace in a body to receive them. The first ship to be honoured in this way was the famous submarine, H.M.S. *Torbay*, whose captain, Commander Miers, received the V.C. Afterwards the same system was extended to the Army; and sometimes as many as a dozen officers and men of one regiment were decorated together, the usual order of precedence at the investitures, by seniority of decoration, being suspended so that the men could follow their officers immediately.

Once or twice special circumstances made some variation of procedure necessary. In 1943, while the King was with his armies in North Africa (and bestowing some decorations there), the Queen held an investiture in his stead, decorating 255 officers and men; and the Duke of Gloucester deputized for the King at an investiture on December 7. In June, 1944, shortly after four investitures and three presentations of medals had been cancelled because of the flying bombs, investitures were held at the Palace of Holyrood in Edinburgh, the first of their kind conducted by a sovereign in wartime for centuries. In October,

the functions at Buckingham Palace were resumed, and on December 6 one of the most notable of all investitures took place when, in the presence of the Queen, General Brereton, Commander-in-Chief of the Allied Airborne Army, General Browning, father of the British Airborne Forces, and 400 of their men, the King decorated the heroes of the gallant attack on Arnhem. Afterwards he and the Queen inspected them, drawn up in the Grand Hall of the Palace.

☆   ☆   ☆

THE precautions always taken to preserve the secrecy of the King's movements were never more elaborate than on his first departure from London during the war. Although presumably the engine driver had some inkling of his destination, even the crew of the royal train were not told where they were going. They were, in fact, bound for the farthest north, where the King was to visit the Home Fleet at their remote anchorage in Scapa Flow. The chief reason for the additional measures of secrecy derived from memories of the tragic sequel to Lord Kitchener's visit to Scapa on his way to Russia in 1916; and soon afterwards they were abundantly justified when a German submarine actually penetrated into Scapa Flow and sank H.M.S. *Royal Oak*. Press correspondents who generally followed the royal progresses were left behind, and the King's journey remained a secret until after his return to London.

This was the first of six visits that the King made to the Fleet in Scapa during the war. On later occasions, however, the advance precautions were relaxed, and wide publicity was subsequently given to the proceedings, for public imagination was stirred by the knowledge that lurking U-boats and constant danger from air attack could not prevent the King of England from going to sea. Each visit lasted about three and a half days and was designed to show the King a different side of the activities of his Navy. Once he led the Fleet to sea for gunnery exercises, standing on the Admiral's bridge of H.M.S. *Duke of York* with Admiral Sir Bruce Fraser at his side, and watched the 14-in. guns firing with great accuracy at target cruisers ten miles away. On another occasion he was borne in the aircraft-carrier *Victorious* to see the men of the Fleet Air Arm repeat the brilliant tactical manoeuvres they had used a week or two previously at the expense of the *Tirpitz*. He saw the newest weapons of under-sea warfare, known to civilians as midget submarines and human torpedoes, and to the Navy as X craft and chariots, went out in a destroyer to chase an imaginary U-boat, and generally took part in all possible activities of the Navy while they waited at Scapa for the enemy who did not come.

The King enjoyed each visit in a different way. Once a seaman always a seaman; and the royal veteran of the battle of Jutland is instantly at home once he is piped over the side of one of his ships. Naval customs and traditions, all of which are second nature to him, are as dear to him as to any other naval officer; and, like his father before him, he loves to see the old ways of the service maintained, and traditional methods of work adapted to the different tasks of seafaring life today. Whether drinking a glass of sherry with the officers in the ward-room or talking strategy and naval politics with the Commander-in-Chief and his staff in the Admiral's cabin, he is equally at ease in the environment of his own profession.

The Navy also thoroughly enjoyed the royal visits, without in any way compromising the seaman's birthright to grumble loudly at the amount of ceremonial drill and painting ship that they entailed. The growls were silenced before the actual visit began, and as the green-and-white " Admiral's Barge," which today is a high-speed motor launch, came alongside ship after ship, every man aboard felt his pride in his Sovereign's presence enhanced by the work he himself had done to make the ship worthy of the occasion. Those who were fortunate enough to have spoken to the King or even to have overheard his conversation with the officers were sure of an audience on the mess decks for many nights to come.

Whenever the King was afloat, guardships patrolled the flagship where he stayed, and in the destroyers guns were loaded and manned, with A.A. defences always on the alert. Although what the King came to watch could only be rehearsal for war, it could never be forgotten that the reality might break upon the Fleet at any moment. Every man believed that the King would have been as delighted as any of them if the guns of the *Duke of York* were firing at hostile battleships instead of our own target cruisers. There is no doubt that the psychological effect of

BUCKINGHAM PALACE, SEPTEMBER, 1940

THE DUKE OF GLOUCESTER SEES WORK OF THE ROYAL OBSERVER CORPS

the royal visits on the naval war was considerable. Three hundred years ago England fought a war one of the professed objects of which was to compel all foreign ships to dip their colours to the English flag in the seas adjoining the British Isles. Today no foreign colours were visible on the North Sea; but the Royal Banner (or Standard, as it is popularly called) flew on the flagship as the King of England sailed proudly and openly to and fro, leading his Fleet where he wished while the great German battleships lay in hiding in the fjords of Norway or closely guarded in their home ports. This was the demonstration of sea power, unshaken since Trafalgar; and every sailor in the Fleet felt the pride of the inheritance as he saw the Royal Banner flying and joined in the cheers as the King's ship passed.

The visits to the Fleet introduced the King to unaccustomed means of conveyance. When he went to the north in August, 1941, and gave the accolade of knighthood to the Commander-in-Chief, Admiral Tovey, in his cabin in the *King George V*, he finished the journey by air, with an escort of fighters. This was the first time a King of England had flown to his Fleet. Normally distinguished visitors are carried in destroyers between the mainland and Scapa, but in June, 1942, when the King was due to leave the Fleet, there was such a sea running that the weather was ruled unsafe for destroyers. Almost at the last minute, therefore, arrangements were made for the King to travel in the *Morialta*, a small steamer built for coastwise trading in Australia, and now used as a liberty boat for ratings. So, for the first time on such an occasion, the Royal Banner flew from a merchantman; and from her bridge, after sailing between the lines of great warships, the King sent the traditional signal of farewell to " splice the mainbrace."

The lighter side of naval life had every encouragement during the King's visits, and he never failed to intersperse his inspections with attendances among his officers and men at concerts in the Fleet theatre on Lyonesse, or at film shows in the ward-rooms after dark when the command was given " hands to dance and skylark." He was with the Navy, however, on many more strenuous occasions. He crossed from Africa in a cruiser, H.M.S. *Aurora*, to meet the victorious garrison and people of Malta in June, 1943; and in another cruiser, H.M.S. *Arethusa*, he visited the Allied bridgehead in Normandy on June 16, 1944, only ten days after the first foothold had been won. It was a Hunt class destroyer, H.M.S. *Garth*, that brought the King safely home in the autumn of 1944, after his visit to the Twenty-first Army Group in the Low Countries, the weather having thwarted his original plan to fly back. These visits to the invading army had been preceded by two days of detailed inspection of final preparations in English harbours, during which the King met his naval commanders in their highly secret invasion headquarters on the south coast and discussed the final plans for the greatest of all amphibious operations. In this decisive phase of the war he was taking real risks both by land and sea; the comparative security of Scapa Flow in the early days could not be expected to be reproduced on the exposed shores of the Channel; and when the King crossed the sea, though his ship was well guarded by accompanying destroyers and aircraft, it was always open to attack in waters where the enemy daily made his presence known. Happily all the royal journeys were completed without untoward incident.

☆　　☆　　☆

THERE is no need to disguise the fact that the Navy holds a special place in the King's heart, which, indeed, it has enjoyed from time immemorial in the affections of the people. He maintained, however, throughout the war, the closest possible touch with all the three Services of which he is the head; and actually his visits to the Army were the most numerous. This, indeed, reflects

THE KING AND QUEEN VISIT A BOMBER STATION, 1941

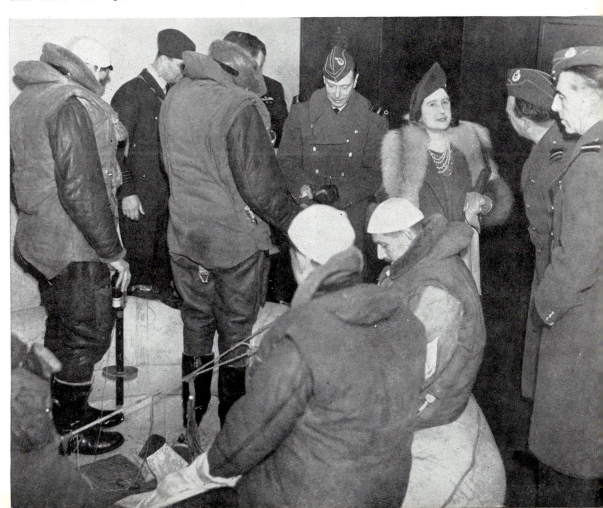

AN OPEN-AIR INVESTITURE AT BUCKINGHAM PALACE, 1940

the fact that the Army is in point of numbers the largest of the three. Although the King was with his troops at every stage of the war, there are three groups of visits to military establishments at home which are of predominant importance; first, the inspections of the original British Expeditionary Force; secondly, the sombre occasions on which he moved among the remnants that came out of Dunkirk, a heart-rending experience for the King, but a source of fresh encouragement to the lacerated but undefeated Army; and thirdly, the tours before the invasion of Europe, when the King inspected division after division, spending a day with each. He watched them at battle practice, sometimes sheltered in sand-bagged emplacements while live shells whistled overhead, examined their new equipment with a skilled and interested eye, for he had experimented with much of it himself at Buckingham Palace, and saw the testing of new tanks and vehicles, of new guns and instruments of gunnery control. Since the King was travelling through areas to which civilians were not admitted, his chauffeur and his valet both entered the Army and were trained, one in the Royal Horse Guards and the other in the Grenadiers. He himself carried a Sten gun concealed in a dispatch case whenever he travelled, that he might be ready at any moment to help in dealing with German parachutists if they should drop in his path and attempt to capture him.

The Army has an instinct for formality, and there was at first a tendency to maintain, on these royal visits, the rigidity of the barrack square. The King, however, soon set himself to break through the crust of ceremonial. Perceiving that, for men who had spent several days in busy preparation for his visit, who had stood on parade for several hours, perhaps in the wet or the cold, before his arrival, the true reward was a direct sight of their Sovereign, he instituted a new kind of royal inspection, in which all was designed so that he should not only see the troops but as many as possible of them should see him. To this end, long lines of men were paraded along each side of country roads, and the King, leaving his car, would walk mile after mile between their ranks, pausing at the end of each company or battalion while the men gave three cheers for him. By the spontaneous heartiness of those cheers they indicated their appreciation of what they had been able

to see for themselves, that the King had put himself to some trouble and inconvenience. It was a sign of his characteristic attention to detail that he ordered that men like the cooks, who are usually left out of formal inspections, should be included in these parades.

When the intensity of preparation increased and the battle schools opened, the King had the opportunity to watch his soldiers rehearsing under the most realistic conditions the attacks they were to deliver in Normandy. This, far more than the ceremonial parades of earlier days, was the kind of contact with the life of a modern army that he enjoyed. New weapons constantly interested him. He would ask soldiers how they liked the new Sten gun, or what they thought of the new bayonet; he would cross-examine officers about the adequacy of supplies, comparing their answers with what he had been told at the factories and depots, and sometimes privately passing on complaints of slow delivery, with the result that a regiment would find its demands met with sudden and startling promptitude. New equipment and devices did not always work perfectly when the King was looking on. Nerves, on such occasions, were apt to be strained, and in the atmosphere of general anxiety the best-laid schemes might gang agley. But minor disasters, such as the complete failure of an early water-proofed vehicle to pass through the test stream that it should have waded with ease, never perturbed the King, to whose sense of humour such unexpected accidents strongly appealed. A friendly smile and a word of encouragement would put the over-anxious young officer or N.C.O. at ease, and at the second attempt the demonstration would generally go off without a hitch.

In the secrecy of a remote Highland loch, the King one day, accompanied by the Queen, boarded a very strange craft. It was the first of the invasion barges, afterwards to become both famous and familiar; and from it the King watched the men of Combined Operations go through one of the very early exercises in landing upon a defended beach. This was long before even the assault on North Africa. Step by step, as the Allied plans developed, the King followed their progress, insisting especially on seeing every new device for himself, and studying every new tactical manoeuvre that was planned. Airborne troops and their new ways of war were a source of

INVESTITURE ON THE FIELD, FRANCE, 1944

inexhaustible interest to him, and the royal visit to General Browning and his men at their secret headquarters a hundred miles from London was the occasion to make public for the first time that Britain possessed an army of the skies. In a barely furnished hut the King and Queen stood listening while the General and his Chief-of-Staff explained a detailed plan for an invasion of France with the aid of a relief map of an area in Normandy, though not of that in which the actual blow was to fall in June, 1944. The exposition of the precise time-table for the drop of the parachute troops, followed by the glider-borne reinforcements, the hours laid down for carrying each successive objective, with exact calculations of the strength of the German defences, sounded at times like a flight of optimistic imagination. The King, however, knew how astonishing had been the building up of the British armies during the defensive years and could appreciate the solid realities on which the prophecy was based. After that there were several royal visits to the airborne forces, and the King made himself familiar with the whole training and tactics of this new mode of war, so that later on, in the great and bitter days of the Sicilian and Norman campaigns, and still later during the heroic battle of Arnhem, he was better able than many professional soldiers to grasp the situation as it showed itself to the airborne commander.

The King, as head of the British Empire, was always specially anxious to see what he could of his troops from overseas. He had few opportunities to meet the men of Australia, New Zealand and South Africa except on his tours abroad; but the Canadians, who began to arrive

AIRBORNE TROOPS, 1944. *Inspecting medical supplies and their containers*

GENERAL SIR MILES DEMPSEY RECEIVES THE ACCOLADE OF KNIGHTHOOD, FRANCE, 1944

ABOARD H.M.S. *DUKE OF YORK*—ENTERING A GUN TURRET 1943

in large numbers in the very early stages of the war, had their full share of his attention. Many times the troops of the Dominion were inspected by the King of Canada on the Aldershot Plain; and the Queen, who is Colonel-in-Chief of the Toronto Scottish, accompanied him on several of these visits. From time to time, also, he was able to meet men from the West Indies and other parts of the Colonial Empire.

The King made, in all, five visits to the battle zones, if the Maginot Line in the days of the early lull can be accounted one of them. The other expeditions were made to North Africa, to Italy, to Normandy, and finally to Belgium and the Netherlands. These were the times when the King saw most of his soldiers, and came more closely into contact with the men who were fighting his battles than any sovereign since George II, who, at Dettingen, was the last King of England to lead his troops in battle. That was in June, 1743. In June, 1943, King George VI flew in great secrecy to Africa, where he inspected units of the British, American, and Free French forces who had just cleared the continent of the enemy, and decorated

General Eisenhower with the G.C.B. He saw men at work and at play. One of the pleasantest scenes, and in its significance one of the most moving, occurred on a beach where he found 3,000 British soldiers revelling in a swim after the hot and dusty warfare of the desert. They ran up from the water, dripping as they were, to surround the King, lustily cheering, or singing the National Anthem. A good deal had changed in the Army since the days of stiff and formal warfare in which George II delighted; but loyalty is capable of very diverse expressions across the centuries while still remaining its essential self. These occasions of easy intercourse between the Sovereign and the rank and file alternated with long hours spent in conference in Cairo with the Allied war leaders, including General Alexander and the Secretaries of State for War and Air—Sir James Grigg and Sir Archibald Sinclair—who had flown out from England with the King.

A few days before D-Day, the King made the last of his visits to the British Army of invasion before it embarked for France. During a long day of inspections of beach parties, commandos,

GOD-SPEED VISIT TO H.M.S. *GEORGE V*, 1944

WITH MEN OF THE MERCHANT NAVY, 1944

MEN OF THE DRIFTERS, 1942

"HUMAN TORPEDO" CREWS, 1944

ABOARD U.S.S. *WASHINGTON*, 1942

and various other units of the Twenty-first Army Group, he lunched with General Montgomery in Rommel's captured caravan, studied the large-scale invasion maps, heard the latest details of the great plan, and afterwards delighted the Commander-in-Chief by decorating his driver with the Military Medal.

A fortnight later, the King and the General met again, for ten days after the landing the King went ashore from a " duck " to inspect the British armies in the field. It was a brisk and business-like visit, devoid of all ceremonial and lasting only a few hours; but the King had time to drive up to advanced headquarters, to study the battle reports coming in from the front line only six miles away, and to hold an open-air investiture. Hundreds of soldiers fresh from battle stood in crowded lines to watch him decorate a number of officers and men. As he crossed the Channel for this visit to the Army, the King had such a view of the panoply of sea power as no other monarch in history has enjoyed.

INSPECTING CROSS-CHANNEL CONTROL, 1944

From the bridge of the cruiser *Arethusa* he could look out on the double line of traffic, tugs, landing craft, merchantmen, and men-of-war, stretching almost unbroken from the English to the Norman shore, and incessantly engaged in the infinitely elaborate process of carrying and convoying a greater and more various armament than had ever been launched in the face of hostile power across the sea.

In the midst of the high drama of the invasion of Normandy the King did not forget that British armies, treading for the first time in the path of so many historic conquerors, had marched victorious into the Eternal City of Rome. At the first opportunity he flew off to Italy to carry them his greetings and congratulations. He did not himself enter Rome, thereby by implication observing a scrupulous courtesy towards King Victor Emmanuel, now his co-belligerent, whose capital it was, but who had not yet himself re-entered it. King George, moreover, was not making his journey in order to visit Italy, or even to

THE QUEEN INSPECTS A W.R.N.S. BOAT CREW, 1942

triumph over the defeated enemy, but rather to meet again his own armies from every part of his Empire, and those of his American ally, in the field. So the great royal plane circled high above the illustrious city, and the King spent the whole of his available time with the armies. Once more he showed in a marked manner his consideration for the men. Mile after mile he drove along the dusty roads in an open car, that all of them might see him, until at night his face was white and his clothes impregnated with dust. The men, who knew those roads and knew also that nothing would have been simpler than for the King to use a closed car, understood and cheered the gesture. The King went to the battlefields, drove past the ruins of the great Abbey of Monte Cassino, stood on a high point with Field-Marshal Alexander to watch a pitched battle in progress beneath him, and came back to England full of admiration for the relentless determination and endurance with which his men were fighting their long battle up the peninsula towards the mountain ramparts of the German fortress.

On the last of the King's visits to the Army during the war in Europe he found the famous Twenty-first Army Group stretched in full line of battle across Belgium and the Netherlands. For four nights he slept in one of the two captured caravans that General Montgomery used as his advanced headquarters. The word " advanced " in these days was not lightly used, for headquarters were now in the pleasant little town of Eindhoven, in the middle of the narrow corridor that Montgomery's men were pushing out into Germany itself, with the rumble of the guns sounding nightly from the enemy only a few miles on either side of where the King lay.

On this expedition the King wore battle-dress for the first time. As in Italy, he abstained from entering the capital of his captive ally, King

VISITING TROOPS IN SCOTLAND, 1943

CANADIANS RECEIVE THE PRINCESS ROYAL, 1941

Leopold, except when he drove into the outskirts of Brussels in order to board his plane after an inspection in the district. Everywhere in both countries the Royal Banner flew from the radiator of his car, so that all might know it was the King of England who passed. The Dutch people were quick to appreciate the trust reposed in their discretion. They cheered, and shouted: " Lang laeve der Koenig"; but it is believed that no word of the royal visit ever leaked into the German lines. One important day was spent with the First Canadian Army in its position near Antwerp; and here the King held an all-Canadian investiture, and met Prince Charles, the Regent of Belgium, at luncheon with General Simonds. On another, he drove some 200 miles, making more than one detour where bridges had been blown up by the retreating enemy, to visit General Eisenhower at his headquarters in the Ardennes. He lunched with the Supreme Commander and twelve American generals, and heard just how and where the next blow was planned to fall.

Clouds, which made it impossible to give adequate fighter escort to the King's plane, prevented him from returning to England by air.

Instead, he was brought home from Ostend in the care of the Navy.

For the youngest of the three fighting services, which in the course of one generation has rivalled the immemorial glories of its seniors, the King has a particular affection and regard, dating back to days before Spitfire and Hurricane were even dreams in a designer's mind. The wings which he wears on his uniform as Marshal of the Royal Air Force were not " assumed " with the rank on his accession, but were gained after the qualifying examination that ends the full training course of a pilot. It was as a young officer in the newly formed R.A.F. that the future King finished his service in the last war; nearly all the men who commanded the diminutive but superbly efficient Air Force which served him in 1939 were his personal friends, the brother officers of his youth. Several of them had been his instructors. Sir Richard Peirse, the first Commander-in-Chief of Bomber Command, was one of those who taught him to fly; and his personal pilot, Squadron-Leader E. H. Fielden, had sought immediate release from his romantically named appointment as " Captain of the King's Flight " in order to go on active service, which brought him to the rank of Air Commodore with a magnificent record as a " Station-master " in Bomber Command.

Up to the beginning of 1945, the King had devoted at least forty tours expressly to the Royal Air Force, some of them lasting two or three days, and nearly all embracing four or five different stations; he also paid a dozen or more visits to the United States Army Eighth and Ninth Air Forces.

Some of these visits included exciting incidents. Once, in January, 1941, when the King was at luncheon in the officers' mess at Mildenhall, the famous air station in Suffolk, the alarm was sounded and signals flashed, causing as near a semblance of consternation as is ever permitted to ruffle the calm of the R.A.F. German aircraft were coming in to attack the airfield. High officers thought the moment had arrived, which had haunted their dreams ever since the King formed his habit of visiting the front-line stations of the R.A.F., when the enemy would attack the person of the Sovereign. As it happened there was only one hostile plane, probably engaged in reconnaissance; no damage was done and the King seemed to enjoy the adventure a good deal more than his embarrassed hosts. Afterwards, however, all the resources of the Air Ministry were invoked to discover how the news of the King's visit had reached the enemy. They never traced the leakage, and eventually concluded that there had been none. The German plane appeared at that time and place by coincidence, and the pilot never knew what a target had been within

A GUARD OF HONOUR AT BELFAST, 1942

his range. But thereafter precautions were intensified, and only a few of the highest officers at any station ever had an inkling of a forthcoming visit from the eminent personage aptly known in the code as " Mr. Lion."

Drama of a lighter character entertained the King on a night that he spent at Mareham, the Bomber Station near King's Lynn. Plans had been laid for what then ranked as a big raid on Cologne, small indeed measured by the standards of later years, but thrilling to all engaged at a time when every raid seemed almost an impudent trespass on the aerial territory ruled by the lords of the Luftwaffe. The King came to hear the pilots briefed, saw them climb into the waiting Wellingtons, and, from the control tower, watched them take off. Then followed a moment of keen amusement in the control tower, as the voice of an irritable pilot came loud and clear over the amplifiers, asking with a torrent of the richest and ripest oaths where the hell was the rear-gunner, as he checked the " inter-com " with each member of the crew. The King, who knows most of the resources of the King's English, grinned.

Later, the King met the pilots and crews on their return in the early morning, and heard for the first time descriptions of Germany as seen from the night sky. Some of the planes he saw take off, however, had been out on an easier mission. Their crews consisted of what R.A.F. slang calls " makee-learns," sent out on their first bombing raid, with orders to attack German installations on the French coast. On this occasion they brought their bomb-racks back full, for weather had prevented clear identification of their targets, and R.A.F. instructions were strict that French lives and property were not to be endangered.

All departments of the air war, as conducted from home airfields, came successively under the royal eye. The King saw the Battle of Britain, as has been said above, from the viewpoint of the fighter stations. Later, at a night fighter station at Middle Wallop, he heard from another group of pilots about an essential part of the system of defence, the counter-attacks that pursued the German raiders homeward through the night sky. He also saw Fighter Command on the offensive, as on a day early in 1942, when he watched fast fighters taking off from Biggin Hill and Kenley for a " rhubarb." This

AUSTRALIANS' GUNNERY EXERCISE, 1940

INSPECTION OF A R.A.F. REGIMENT IN NORTH AFRICA, 1943

vegetable symbolized to the informed R.A.F. mind a sweep upon German rail communications in France. Although Coastal Command, partaking of the character of the " silent " service with which it collaborated, was seldom heard of by the laity, the King's frequent visits showed his sense of the vast importance of the part played by its members in guarding the dangerous sea zones round the British Isles, through which passed the traffic that sustained the life of the nation, and in which it was perfectly possible for the war to be lost. Besides visits to Coastal Command Headquarters and several coast stations, his travels extended as far as Scotland, where he and the Queen went in December, 1942, to see the gigantic airport at Prestwick and be shown by Transport Command the complex organization that brought in thousands of aircraft from across the Atlantic.

All the new technicalities of the air were of great interest to the King, who discussed the latest developments with Sir Charles Portal, the other heads of the Service, and the specialists who could give him first-hand descriptions of every new device. Directly he heard of the introduction

of " Pathfinder " bombing, the King asked to go and see the men and their new equipment. In East Anglia early in 1942 he was shown the " Master Bomber " Lancasters at three big stations, discussed them at length with Air Marshal Bennet, the originator and commander of the " Pathfinders," and saw demonstrations of the very secret marking flares and other pinpointing devices. Officers led the royal party up to the window of the operations room and invited them to look across the great airfield, while an elaborate array of switches and controls was manipulated in the background. In a few moments a thick wall of fire sprang up along the whole length of the runways where the bombers were to make their landings; and in a few minutes a fog, which would have made landing dangerous, was dispersed, so that home-coming bombers could land in safety. Thus the King and Queen were the first two people outside the men actually responsible for the work, to see in operation FIDO, the fog disperser, one of the greatest life-saving secrets of the war, representing a supreme triumph of research, at once patient and urgent, over difficulties that for long seemed insuperable.

Another secret first shown to the King at an R.A.F. station in Yorkshire was the work of his new parachute troops. Group-Captain Pickard, famous as the Captain of "F for Freddie," who had been a pioneer in the perfection of the parachute drop, was with him and the Queen when hundreds of the new air warriors dropped out of their planes, floated to the ground, and immediately ran over to form up in front of the King with precision reminiscent of the Horse Guards Parade. Then, at a remote station on the Norfolk coast, the King and Queen went out on the fore-shore, and presently were deafened as Typhoons roared across at over 300 miles an hour. These machines were carrying something set down on the royal programme under the uninformative name of "F.M.No. ——." It was in fact the new and highly secret rocket of the R.A.F.; and the sudden high-pitched scream of the projectiles, speeding on from the fast-moving planes, to ex-plode with a shattering noise as they hit the surface, was an exciting experience even for the King.

The King was, of course, kept informed about all new aircraft approved by the Air Council for production; and either at the factory, where the prototypes were carefully hidden behind high wooden screens, or on the experimental airfield, he was shown each new British plane as it came into being. He and the Queen received a particularly dramatic demonstration when they came out after tea in the mess of an R.A.F. station, and there flashed over their heads, as they stood in the road-way, the fastest twin-engined plane in the world, the new wooden-bodied Mosquito. The testing pilot threw his machine about the sky in an astonishing series of dizzy manoeuvres, then shot off into the distance at a speed of over 400 miles an hour. Before the royal party had recovered their breath he was back, this time flying more slowly, to repeat the whole series of tricks and turns with one air-screw "feathered," the plane flying on a

LUNCHEON ON THE FIELD, NORTH AFRICA, 1943. *The King's companions are Sir James Grigg, Secretary of State for War, and the American Generals Clark and Patton*

THANKSGIVING FOR NORTH AFRICAN VICTORY, 1943

single engine, a feat hitherto regarded as quite impossible for a twin-engined aircraft.

Proudly as the R.A.F. has welcomed the King on all his visits to its stations, it particularly treasures the memory of the personal service it has been able to give him. For his expeditions to Africa, to Italy, and to the Netherlands, the King chose air transport; and when he travelled by sea the R.A.F. was always in attendance, its squadrons

THE GEORGE CROSS

of fighters weaving overhead for his protection. Even on the royal journeys by train, in days when German bombers were almost daily over England, it was not uncommon for the fighters to fly on guard up and down the line as the King passed.

☆　　☆　　☆

INTERSPERSED with all these visits to the fighting services, the unending routine of kingship went on. There were royal broadcasts at Christmas and on other significant occasions,

notably one in September, 1940, when the King addressed the Empire from its capital, then suffering the full fury of the air assault. This was an assurance to all the Dominions that the Mother Country, however terribly its ordeal might develop, would not fail the Commonwealth. The following month Princess Elizabeth, then aged fourteen, spoke to all the British children who had been sent overseas for safety, giving them a message of courage and confidence from all the children who had remained at home. "It was perfectly done," the South African novelist, Sarah Gertrude Millin, wrote in her diary. "If there are still queens in the world a generation hence, this child will be a good queen."

Important foreign visitors, representatives of their peoples, as the King and Queen represent those of the British Commonwealth, were entertained at Buckingham Palace. There was Mr. Wendell Willkie, bringing messages of cordial friendship from the still neutral United States, and from his former opponent, President Roosevelt. Later on Mrs. Roosevelt, whose frank and vigorous personality had greatly attracted the King and Queen when they met her in the United States, paid them a return visit. Coming as she did as a kind of informal and peculiarly confidential ambassador from her distinguished husband, she speedily won a secure place in the hearts of the British people. At Buckingham Palace she was remembered as one of the most welcome of guests; she created a remarkable precedent by continuing her famous newspaper column, "My Day," from inside the walls of the King's home. Her authentic accounts of life at the Palace, and her graphic descriptions of the devastation that her royal hosts showed her in London, were eagerly read throughout the United States. In March, 1941, General de Gaulle, who was just achieving recognition as leader of the Fighting French, was received by the King at the Palace; and in July of that year a formal reception was given to the heads of all the allied states who were living in exile in London and to the members of their governments.

No guest was more welcome than Field-Marshal Smuts, the most famous veteran in the Empire, who came to London to assist with the invasion plans in the autumn of 1943, and stayed the week-end with the King and Queen at Windsor Castle;

MALTA, 1943

IN THE STREETS OF SENGLEA, MALTA, 1943

WITH GENERAL ALEXANDER
IN ITALY, 1944

A FORWARD OBSERVATION POST, NORTH OF AREZZO, 1944

he was also present at a party for 500 officers from the Dominions at Buckingham Palace, where the Princesses helped their parents to entertain the guests. The following year, on the eve of the expedition to Normandy, the King and Queen gave a dinner to the Prime Ministers of the Dominions, who were assembled for conference in London. Other guests from remote regions were the Regent of Iraq, and the Chinese Goodwill Mission, headed by Professor Wang Shihchieh.

Though all the pomp and circumstance of royalty had been laid aside at the outbreak of war, certain ceremonies of constitutional importance were inconspicuously continued. Chief among these was the royal opening of each annual session of Parliament. On these occasions the King and Queen drove to the Palace of Westminster in a closed car, instead of in the horse-drawn landau of peace. But the suspension of pageantry did not affect the essence of the ancient function, even when, after the Houses themselves had been bombed, Parliament met in strange surroundings at Church House, Westminster, and the King and Queen sat on extemporized and apparently precarious thrones.

Every day throughout the war the King's Guard was mounted at the Palace; and although the red coats and bearskins of peace had been put away in the quartermaster's stores, the less spectacular khaki and steel helmets indicated that the Guard was much more of a business-like precaution than

LORD LOVAT'S COMMANDO PARADES BEFORE THE LANDING IN NORMANDY, 1944

the ceremonial formality that it seemed in ordinary days. From time to time the Brigade of Guards handed over their cherished duties to other units whom the King wished to honour; and on these occasions the King and Queen themselves generally came into the forecourt to see the Guard changed. The new R.A.F. Regiment, for instance, mounted the Guard on the twenty-fifth anniversary of the foundation of the R.A.F., and so did the Home Guard on its own third anniversary; and it was a great hour for the men of the Westminster Battalion, many of whom were recruited from the clerical and domestic staff at the Palace, when, in the presence of the King and Queen, the keys were handed to one of their officers, and they were left for twenty-four hours responsible for the King's safety.

Other ceremonies, of which the solemnity was in no way affected by the absence of spectacular trappings, were the various critical or joyous occasions on which the King officially represented his peoples at prayer. The first great thanksgiving service of the war was held by the King's order at St. Paul's after the final defeat of Rommel in Africa by British and American troops; and both the King and the Queen attended it before he left to visit the victorious army. Another, to commemorate the Battle of Britain, took place at the third anniversary in September, 1943. At the most anxious moment in the later stages of the war, on the first Sunday of the invasion of Europe, the King and Queen again took their place at the head of the nation at a solemn service of intercession in Westminster Abbey.

TOURING INVASION BEACHES, 1944

IN THE MAP LORRY AT FIELD-MARSHAL MONTGOMERY'S H.Q. IN HOLLAND, 1944

All through the war the royal train was steaming hither and thither, as the effort of war production became every month more extensive. More and more great industrial colonies were growing up in the national service, and deserved and received the encouragement of a visit from the King and Queen. They travelled backwards and forwards through Scotland and Wales, Lancashire and Yorkshire, to the old dockyard towns of Chatham and Portsmouth, to Cornwall and Devon, to the Midlands and Manchester; and everywhere they walked through miles of war factories, and studied the intricate processes of making air-craft, tanks, guns, shells, plastic bombs, field-glasses, electric gear, ships, uniforms, medicines and every kind of war material. These factory visits followed no formal pattern, and to the King the very heart of them was in the long talks in which he engaged the work-people themselves. In the factories he was very much at home; for in his youth as Duke of York, when he had no direct prospect of accession to the Throne, he had made himself the special authority in the royal family on industrial affairs; and as President of the Industrial Welfare Society had learned to know the life and outlook of the men and women at the benches, the looms and the lathes. Now, on his tours of the war factories, he was moving among people whom he understood and appreci-ated. The Queen, with her natural friendliness and ability to put all kinds of people at their ease, received the confidences of thousands of women and girls in the midst of the clang of the machinery or at their meals in the factory canteen.

Production practically ceased for several hours on all these visits. Urgent requests or orders were issued that work must go on as usual, but human nature would not be denied, and men and women ran from their benches to see the royal visitors, or crowded along the factory lines to cheer. After the King and Queen had passed there were hours of talk about the visit; so that inevitably

WITH GENERAL EISENHOWER, FRANCE, 1944

IN THE NETHERLANDS, 1944

less work was done than on any other day of the year. At one time, when every moment of possible work was precious, the Ministry of Supply made a statistical study of the effect of the King's visits on production. Scores of different types of factory were included in the survey; but in every case the same results were found. Figures of production dropped sharply on the day of the visit, and sometimes on the day before. The weekly figures, however, invariably rose; renewed vigour was instilled into the work when the men and women saw that they had the personal interest of the King and Queen; and, far from desiring the royal visits to be curtailed, the production authorities were only anxious to have more and more of them.

The King and Queen lunched frequently in the canteens, and on each visit asked for a ten minutes' break for a cup of tea in the morning, over which the King would hear from the factory managers the inside story of the increased production figures he had perhaps been shown before he came. For in a sense he was making his inspections as Chairman of the universal parent company, since all the factories were working for the nation; but in another sense he came as representative of everybody outside the factories, and especially of the fighting services of which he was the head, to express their gratitude for the prodigious and sustained efforts being put forth within. Somewhere in the royal archives is a list of all the factories the King and Queen visited. It reads like a comprehensive index to the whole industrial life of Great Britain at war. Never once in these hundreds of visits did the King or Queen scamp an inspection, or allow fierce heat, noisome smells, or other unpleasant conditions to deter them from seeing every relevant detail. Many times the time-table went awry, and anxious railway officials fussed over schedules while the royal train, to which other traffic must give way, waited in the station for the return of the King and

Queen. But this was always because the King, or more frequently the Queen, who, like most women, believes that time-tables are made for men and not men for time-tables, had become so interested in the work they saw, or so sympathetic with the stories they heard, that at the end of a long and tiring day they stayed longer at a factory or a rest centre than the programme allowed.

New ideas, solutions to the new problems of wartime nursery schools, workers' canteens, and all else that could make the daily life of the people easier, were a never failing source of interest to the Queen. Her first anxiety when she visited a new place or a new factory, a bombed area or an evacuation centre, was to know how the mothers and their families were faring, who was looking after them and how, and what more was needed to provide for their welfare.

Wherever war work went on in the busy shipyards of the Clyde, in the sweltering blast furnaces of the north, in vast new ordnance factories, the King and Queen went. Nor did they ask for exemptions from the rules their subjects had to obey. When a conscientious sentry challenged the King on a night visit to a munitions factory in London, the King complied with orders and produced his identity card. At home all the royal family had their ration cards, and ate their weekly allowances, and no more, of meat, sugar, tea and the rest. The Queen frequently inquired from the Palace kitchen for assurance that their rations were not being exceeded. On a visit to the Ministry of Food she revealed that, like other families, the four of them pooled their meat coupons for a week-end joint; and when there was a party at the Palace, however official or important, applications were made on the appointed

WITH THE R.A.F. IN BELGIUM, 1944

The King meets the late Wing-Commander Guy Gibson, V.C., on his return from leading the successful raid by R.A.F. bombers on the great Ruhr dams in May, 1943

THE DUCHESS OF KENT WATCHES AMERICAN AIRMEN RETURN FROM A RAID, 1945

forms to the Westminster Food Office for permission to buy additional supplies of tea or biscuits. The royal family also had their clothing coupons; but the Queen bought very few new clothes during the war, being content for the most part with the wardrobe she had bought for the Canadian tour of 1939, and the King wore civilian clothes at week-ends only.

☆   ☆   ☆

THE primary royal duty of acting as a focus of unity for all the peoples of Great Britain and the Commonwealth, is diffused in a secondary measure over all the members of the royal family. Each of them, except the very youngest children, had his or her special function during the war. It will be remembered that at the beginning the heiress presumptive, Princess Elizabeth, was only thirteen and a half, and not yet qualified

by law to take any part in the formal duties of her rank.

Whenever the King was absent from the realm, a recent Act of Parliament ordained that his place should be supplied by a Council of State consisting of the Queen and the next four adults in the line of succession. This Council had to act on five different occasions, its composition varying slightly as some members of the royal family grew up and others died. In the days when the King was sharing all the dangers of his people in bombed London, serious account had also to be taken of the possibility of his sudden death. If that grievous blow had fallen upon the country before Princess Elizabeth had reached the age of eighteen, a Regency would have been required by law and would have fallen upon the King's next brother, the Duke of Gloucester; and it was therefore thought desirable that, after his return from the first campaign in France in 1940, the Duke should not again leave England until

AT A NORTHERN BASE, 1942

the Princess reached the age of eighteen on April 21, 1944. As that birthday approached a curious gap in the law was discovered; for, although she was capable of reigning as Queen at the age of eighteen, she could not be Regent during an illness of her father until she came of age at twenty-one. A Bill was passed through Parliament to correct this anomaly, so that henceforth the Princess was not only the King's destined successor, but his deputy whenever one was required. Until 1944, however, the Duke of Gloucester remained always near the King in order to be available as his understudy; and he fulfilled, with little publicity, an arduous round of royal duties, mainly in connexion with the Army.

Every member of the royal family took part in war service; and their names appeared in all sections of the casualty lists, killed, wounded, and prisoners. The first place of honour belongs to the Duke of Kent, who died on active service.

The Duke's service was varied and arduous. On the outbreak of war he immediately decided to postpone his departure to take up the great imperial office of Governor General of the Commonwealth of Australia, to which the Australian Cabinet of Mr. Menzies had asked the King to appoint him just before the war. He then almost disappeared from public view; he had, in fact, gone to the Admiralty, reverting to the naval service for which he had been trained as a young man. He worked hard, first in London and later at a northern base under Mr. Winston Churchill as First Lord. After a visit of inspection to naval bases in France, he transferred in 1940 to the Ministry of Labour in order to see how the men and women in the factories were faring. He made a series of industrial tours, including a visit to a coal mine at Whitehaven, where he hewed coal alongside the miners. Then at the King's request he rejoined the Royal Air Force, with whose war service no member of the Royal Family had hitherto been associated, laying down his titular rank of Air Vice-Marshal in order to serve as a Group Captain.

In the R.A.F. the Duke did most valuable work as a welfare officer. He flew thousands of miles under war conditions, besides finding time for visits to bombed areas and other royal tasks outside the Service. He was promoted Air Commodore on his merits; and in July, 1941, he

AT THE COVENTRY AND WARWICKSHIRE HOSPITAL

W.A.A.F. GUARD OF HONOUR, 1943

THE PRINCESS ROYAL WITH WOUNDED (*ABOVE*), 1944. A.T.S. ON PARADE (*BELOW*), 1942

became the first member of the royal family to fly the Atlantic. During this flight he himself took for a time the controls of the Liberator in which he travelled.

His purpose was to inspect the great imperial air-training scheme in Canada. After a thorough investigation, he wrote on his return a full report of all that he had seen, which proved of great value to the Air Council. The tour also included a short visit to the United States during which he stayed with President Roosevelt at the White House.

The destination of the Duke's last journey was Iceland, where he was intending to pursue his welfare duties among the British airmen then in occupation. The weather was unfavourable when he reached the Scottish airport from which he was to take off; but all was ready, the Australian crew were anxious to leave, and the Duke was reluctant to waste time. The flying boat took off, circled, and disappeared. The Duke was never seen again alive. Some time later a farm worker in Sutherland heard a machine crash, and, searching the countryside for the wreckage, found the Duke's dead body near by. A few days later the King came from Balmoral to see the spot where his brother had died; but there was nothing he could do, except to seek comfort for the widowed Duchess by sending for her sister, Princess Olga, to come at once to England. Of her three children, Prince Michael had been born during the war, being only seven weeks old. The Duke was buried with royal and military honours at Windsor.

INSPECTING POLISH COLOURS IN THE SCOTTISH COMMAND, 1941

IN THE WOODS AT BADMINTON

It has always been the tradition of the royal family that at least one of its members should make the Army his career. In an earlier generation this part was played by the Duke of Connaught, whose death in 1942 severed a remarkable link in military history, for he was the godson of the great Duke of Wellington, who was born in 1769. The military member of the present King's family is his brother, the Duke of Gloucester, who has from his youth up set himself to become a professional soldier. He saw active service in France as Chief Liaison Officer to the Commander-in-Chief, Lord Gort, throughout the campaign that ended at Dunkirk. After being slightly wounded at Arras, he came home to take up a similar appointment in the Home Forces during the period of re-arming and re-grouping. He had reverted at his own request to the rank of Major-General; but before long the Chief of the Imperial General Staff recommended his promotion to Lieutenant-General in recognition of the great value of his work. In 1941 the Duke was Second-in-Command of the Twentieth Armoured Brigade; then, in the summer of 1942, he undertook one of the longest of royal air tours in order to inspect troops stationed in the Middle East and India.

He visited Gibraltar, Egypt, Libya, the Sudan, Somaliland, Eritrea, Aden, Kenya, Palestine, Syria, Iraq, Persia, India and Ceylon. It was his great ambition to command a division in the field; but on the death of the Duke of Kent the King had to ask him to give up full-time military duties in order that he might become the chief royal deputy.

When the assumption of public duties by Princess Elizabeth released him from the urgency of this work, the Australian Government of Mr. Curtin invited the Duke to fill the place left empty by his brother's death, and come to Canberra as Governor General. The King gave his cordial approval, and the Duke left England, with his wife and children, in December, 1944. In the meantime, he had worked hard visiting war factories, R.A.F. stations, Naval establishments, Civil Defence units, hospitals, and other scenes of war activity, as well as taking a constant interest in the work done under his Prisoners-of-War Fund, and in the permanent youth movements assisted by King George's Jubilee Trust, of which he is Chairman.

There was no reason why Queen Mary should remain in London during its years of danger; and it would certainly have been a cause of acute and unnecessary anxiety to the King if his mother had remained within the area of attack. Her public work for the Empire was done; and she withdrew quietly into retirement at Badminton, the home of the Duke and Duchess of Beaufort. Many men and women of the Services stationed in those

QUEEN MARY'S MEDALLION

parts have pleasant memories of days when, as they walked along the Somersetshire roads, a large motor car would draw up beside them and a dignified old lady sitting in the back would offer them a lift.

Queen Mary would talk to them with kindly interest about their duties; and on setting them down the chauffeur would hand to each a small medallion as a memento of a casual meeting with the Queen Mother of England. But although retired from public life, Queen Mary insisted on offering some war service, and is proud to remember that she and a party of helpers assisted the

THE DUCHESS OF KENT (*ABOVE*), AT A COLLIERY; (*BELOW*), AT A SERVICE CLUB

THE DUCHESS OF GLOUCESTER OPENING A CLUB FOR SERVICE WOMEN, 1940

land campaign by working nearly every afternoon from two until four, and in the five years cleared 111 acres of woodland.

The younger ladies of the Royal Family divided between them the sphere of the Women's Services. The Princess Royal acted as the honorary head of the A.T.S.; she also presided over the British Red Cross Society, and the R.A.F. Nursing Service bears her name. The Duchess of Kent was chief of the W.R.N.S., in whose welfare she took the liveliest interest throughout the war, and from whom she did not allow the sorrows of widowhood to detach her. The Duchess of Gloucester took a similar place in the W.A.A.F., and was indefatigable in promoting their interests. All three Princesses became familiar figures to the Services with which they were especially associated, while at the same time taking their place in the general round of royal intercourse

with the war life of the country, both service and civilian.

The Princess Royal shared the anxious experience of so many thousands of mothers when her elder son, Lieutenant Viscount Lascelles, of the Grenadier Guards, was taken prisoner by the Germans. Like other prisoners, Lord Lascelles had to depend on Red Cross parcels for very necessary food, and could only write notes of twenty-five words to his parents; the only exceptional treatment he received took the sinister form of being placed, in 1944, together with other allied prisoners of exalted connexions, in a special camp in South Germany, where there was thought to be an intention to use them as hostages in bargaining for the lives of the greater war criminals. If this was ever seriously contemplated, the extreme rapidity of the final American advance thwarted the plan; and the Princess

THE QUEEN AND PRINCESS ELIZABETH VISIT A SCHOOL FOR CRIPPLED CHILDREN, 1945

QUEEN MARY AND THE LORD MAYOR AFTER THANKSGIVING AT ST. PAUL'S, 1945

PRINCESS ELIZABETH, SEA RANGER, 1944

young girls of her age, had several favourite heroes, mostly in the R.A.F. One young fighter pilot will not have forgotten that, when he went to the Palace to receive the D.S.O., the King said: "Princess Elizabeth will be much excited when I tell her I have seen and decorated you; she follows all your adventures." The Princess's first war efforts were in helping to grow vegetables in the royal gardens and to knit woollen comforts for sailors. Her unique position, however, drew her towards special duties long before the age at which she became formally qualified for public functions. When she made her first broadcast to the children of the Empire, she was only fourteen. That was a child's graceful achievement; she might be considered grown up when more than four years later she spoke again on the wireless, this time in French to thank the children of Belgium for their Christmas gift of toys to British children. In these broadcasts she stepped naturally into her predestined position as the representative of the new generation of the Empire.

At sixteen the Princess went to the Labour Exchange at Windsor and there filled in an ordinary registration form for national service, giving the Girl Guides as her sphere of pre-service training. She became the "bosun" of a crew of Sea Rangers recruited from her young friends and the daughters of the Palace staff. By her service here she not only gained valuable experience for herself, but began to help her parents in keeping touch with all the various youth training organizations which gained so large a place in the hopes of the nation during the war. The King and Queen, in the midst of all their other pressing duties, took special care to visit the organizations of youth at every opportunity. One memorable event was the inspection of naval, military and air-force cadet organizations in the quadrangle of Buckingham Palace in July, 1942. Bodies like the Boy Scouts Association had many assurances of the royal interest. The enrolment of the King's own children in a youth service was the most direct declaration the Royal Family could make of their whole-hearted faith in the national movement.

When Princess Elizabeth reached the age of eighteen, and new duties defined by law fell upon her, the King announced his decision that her training as heiress presumptive and her public

Royal and the royal family had the pleasant experience of welcoming Lord Lascelles home at dinner at the Palace on the night before VE-Day.

The King and Queen shared with hosts of other parents the anxiety of watching their children grow up in the strained and unnatural atmosphere of war. Very properly they attempted to protect the two Princesses from the direct impact of the struggle, and to carry on their education with as near to normality as might be. At the outset both Princesses were sent for safety to Balmoral; but later on they spent most of their time at Windsor. Here, under the care of an accomplished Scottish governess, Princess Elizabeth was gradually introduced to a course of study very carefully designed to prepare her for the vast responsibilities she will some day bear. Meanwhile she followed the course of the war in the newspapers and the broadcasts, and, like most

PRINCESS ELIZABETH IN THE A.T.S., 1945

INSPECTING GIRLS' TRAINING CORPS, 1945

THE DUKE OF KENT, KILLED ON ACTIVE SERVICE, 1942

LORD LASCELLES. *Second from the left is Lord Lascelles, who was wounded and taken prisoner on the night of June 18-19, 1944, and released on May 5, 1945*

duties outweighed the claims of ordinary national service. She would not, therefore, enter any of the auxiliary services. The Princess, however, chafed under this decision, and eventually persuaded her father to revoke it. By her own choice he granted her, nearly a year later, an honorary commission as second subaltern in the A.T.S., and she went off at once to a training centre for drivers at Camberley. Here she joined a squad of other girls going through the ordinary N.C.O.'s course, and emerged as a fully qualified driver, celebrating her graduation by driving an army car from Camberley through the thickest of London's afternoon traffic, twice round Piccadilly Circus, and at last triumphantly through the gates of Buckingham Palace.

On her sixteenth birthday, the Princess received the honorary appointment of Colonel of the Grenadier Guards, in which illustrious regiment she has ever since taken a keen and abiding interest, studying its history, following its war exploits in detail, and on several occasions inspecting its battalions at Windsor and elsewhere.

There was a repetition for the King and Queen of some of their tragic experiences of earlier years when they moved among the victims of the flying bombs and rockets in the late summer and autumn of 1944. Once again they themselves were not immune from danger; one day the King walked through the Palace gardens to inspect the damage at Hyde Park Corner, where a flying bomb had fallen during the night. Some amusement was caused among the few who knew the facts, by the newspaper announcement that His Majesty had " inspected wreckage caused by a flying bomb in the South of England," that being the only phrase allowed by the censorship to describe a walk across his own garden.

The mounting hopes and changing character

GOVERNOR GENERAL OF AUSTRALIA. *The Duke of Gloucester is seen with the Governor of Aden on his journey to Australia, of which he was appointed Governor General in November, 1943*

MEMORIAL SERVICE TO PRESIDENT ROOSEVELT, APRIL, 1945

of the war, however, were now being reflected in the royal engagements. After a visit to Scotland in October, 1944, to take leave of the great battleship *King George V* before she sailed to join the British Pacific Fleet—a transfer of power made possible by the destruction of the *Tirpitz*—the King drove to Westminster to open what was already felt to be the last session of the war Parliament. On December 3, he and the Queen went to Hyde Park to attend a parade of great and happy significance, the stand down of the Home Guard, whose weary but essential duty of waiting for the invasion that never came had ended with the disappearance of the enemy's last chance of attack. On December 16, the King and

Queen were at Euston to say goodbye to the Duke and Duchess of Gloucester on their long-postponed departure for Australia. Then, after a series of Christmas visits to service clubs, the King's Christmas Day broadcast closed the eventful record of the invasion year.

The sense of imminent victory was in the air of 1945 from the very beginning. Thousands of flags fluttered all along the route of the royal New Year tour in Lancashire. More great ships, released from their duties of watching the now helpless German navy, were on their way to the East, and the King and Queen went to the ports to see them off. The King dealt with post-war plans such as those for rebuilding his shattered

On the way to St. Paul's after victory, 1945. The Lord Mayor surrenders the City Sword

Palace of Westminster, and spent some time one day walking round the ruins while Mr. Churchill explained the designs for the new House of Commons. At Buckingham Palace the King and Queen received the British delegates who were going to San Francisco to plan the structure of international relations in the post-war world. Next day, however, came the last piece of bad news, and one of the most grievous: that of the death of President Roosevelt. The King sent a telegram of deep and heartfelt sympathy to Mrs. Roosevelt from both himself and the Queen, and ordered Court mourning for a week. This was an unusual tribute to the head of a foreign state; but no foreigner has won a place comparable to Roosevelt's in the hearts of the British people, and the King reflected their universal feeling.

The King was in Norfolk with the Queen when news came of Himmler's offer to surrender to the Western Powers. The Queen had arranged to fly to London for the wedding of her niece, Miss Rosemary Bowes-Lyon, but the King travelled to London at once by train to await developments, and the Queen had to postpone her first flight since the accession until the day, several weeks later when, as Duchess of Normandy, she came home with " The Duke " from the liberated Channel Islands. Very few knew why the King had changed his plans, and several days went by with no outward developments, although a constant stream of papers relating to the rapid spread in Germany of the paralysis of defeat passed before the King in the privacy of his study. On Sunday, May 6, the anniversary of his father's accession, the King was at Windsor when an urgent call came from the Cabinet office. He drove to London with the Queen, and there waited for the expected announcement of unconditional surrender. He was in hourly touch with Mr. Churchill, who kept him constantly informed of the conversations with Moscow, on which the time of the general announcement depended; at 6 p.m. on May 7, however, a decision was taken to postpone it until the morrow.

But all now knew that the announcement was coming, and what it would be. That night crowds began to gather round the Palace, and all through the following day the Mall was black with thronging multitudes of people, all responding to the universal instinct to gather in the hour of victory round the King. Meanwhile, in the afternoon, the official announcement was made by the Prime Minister over the wireless and afterwards repeated by him in the House of Commons and by Lord Woolton in the House of Lords. The King in his room in the Palace listened to this public declaration of the end of the great struggle. All through the early evening the cheering crowds before the Palace grew thicker and thicker; but at nine o'clock the cheering ceased, and the thousands stood in silence to hear from the loud-speakers the King's own broadcast. The world-wide Commonwealth was listening with them. The King's voice went out over the towns and villages of the three kingdoms; to all his ships at sea; to his victorious troops, resting at last in the ruined towns of Germany or the ravaged fields of the lands they had freed; to others still battling in the swamps and jungles of Asia, or among the islands of Far Eastern seas; to men and women listening on the prairies of Canada or the South African veldt, in the winter dawn of Australia and New Zealand; gathered round Indian mosques and temples, or scattered through the vast spaces of the Colonies in Africa, the Caribbean and round the globe. In the direct

THANKSGIVING SUNDAY, MAY 13, 1945

and moving language to which they had become accustomed from his lips, he spoke to them of the splendour of their common achievement, of the blood and tears that had been shed upon the arduous way, of the judgment that had fallen upon the pride and malice of their enemies, of the crowning mercy by which their own faithfulness had been rewarded; and finally of the new hope that dawned with their victory for the tortured millions of mankind.

Afterwards the King and Queen, with their daughters, came out on the balcony above the great entrance to the Palace, while the crowd below sang the National Anthem and cheered and cheered again. Tears stood in the Queen's eyes as she heard them. It was a moment of high and rare emotion such as comes but seldom even in the lives of kings. Out there to the east lay in dishonoured ruins the monstrous dominion whose ruler had declared that it would last a thousand years. In England there had been no such arrogant claim to know or bind the future; only a steadfast hope and the prayer: " Long live the King." But behind the prayer and the hope lay more than a thousand years of continuous and broadening progress in liberty, won by the people of England, and afterwards by the people of the British Empire, under the leadership of forty generations of English kings and queens. Thousands of men and women in that great multitude must have remembered another evening just ten years before, when they had had their last sight of King George V, standing on that same balcony, and modestly rejoicing in the love of his subjects, manifested in the Silver Jubilee and the Indian summer of his reign. Now they knew that they had kept alive, in his son's name, through unimagined perils and labours, the immemorial tradition, for which he in his time had stood, of a nation at unity in itself.

Many times in the course of that and the following evening, the Royal Family came out on the balcony to respond to the unceasing acclamation of the crowd. Once Mr. Churchill came with them, but he was content to stand a little in the background while the King acknowledged the salutes. This was not his hour. Great man as he is, he knew that here he was in the presence of something greater than himself, of the King and people of his country, one and indivisible. Together, more than five years ago, they had dedicated

VICTORY TOUR OF LONDON

themselves to a warfare to the death in defence of all the ideals of justice, freedom, and mercy, in which their national life was rooted. Together they had fought and endured through hardships and dangers that, save to the eye of faith, sometimes seemed insurmountable. Their faith had never wavered; and now King and people were still together in the hour of a victory more complete than they had ever known. In a few days the King would go in state to St. Paul's Cathedral, with the Pearl Sword of the City carried aloft before him, to render thanks on behalf of all his peoples to the Power whose protection he had invoked for their cause in his broadcast on the first day of war. It was right that in such a mingling of majesty and humility the German war should be sacramentally ended. But on this first night of deliverance the universal feeling demanded a more intimate expression of an Empire's gratitude, not to the symbolic Crown, but to the man who had worn it, and by his own devotion magnified its ancient glories, through these terrible years. Down there in the gathering shadows were the dark masses of the people of England; but up on the balcony also, in a true sense, was the people, incarnate in the person of its Head. Not only the people of today, who had won the war, but the people of tomor-

row whose inheritance they had saved; for on the King's right Princess Elizabeth, in her uniform, stood for the future of the Empire and the continuing consecration of royalty to its service. Something of the magic and mystery of monarchy seemed to hover about the little group on the illuminated balcony. Something perhaps even vaster was present to many minds than could be comprehended in the image of the living Empire or of a single member in the endless succession of its kings; for in the high moments of history men may be given a glimpse of the august workings of universal destiny, and a sense that they themselves are greater than they know. But mortality cannot sustain that vision. This was no time to rest in victory, or even to pause for long. Another great war in the East summoned King and people for the continuance of their unwearying struggle. It was to be mercifully short; but none yet knew how soon the exaltation of this night was to be renewed and consummated. The King and Queen withdrew from the balcony for the last time; one by one the windows of the Palace were darkened; the multitudes dispersed quietly upon their homeward way; and the flickering lights which celebrate our earthly victories dwindled and were quenched beneath the changeless radiance of the stars.

VICTORY